Catherine Rothwell's

Lancashire Cookbook

GW00585056

Copyright © Catherine Rothwell, 2000

All Rights Reserved. No part of this publication may be reproduced, stored in a retrieval system, or transmitted in any form or by any means – electronic, mechanical, photocopying, recording, or otherwise – without prior written permission from the publisher or a licence permitting restricted copying issued by the Copyright Licensing Agency, 90 Tottenham Court Road, London W1P 0LA. This book may not be lent, resold, hired out or otherwise disposed of by trade in any form of binding or cover other than that in which it is published, without the prior consent of the publisher.

Published by Sigma Leisure – an imprint of
Sigma Press, 1 South Oak Lane, Wilmslow, Cheshire SK9 6AR, England.

British Library Cataloguing in Publication Data
A CIP record for this book is available from the British Library.

ISBN: 1-85058-718-3

Typesetting and Design by: Sigma Press, Wilmslow, Cheshire.

Cover Design: Design House

Printed by: MFP Design & Print

Preface

Twenty years have elapsed since I wrote "Lancashire Recipes Old and New", a modest book harking back to the days of simple cooking in fire ovens. Since then, what a wind of change has blown through Lancashire's kitchens!

A new generation has arrived with new ideas, for no longer do people remain all their lives in the town where they were born. Greater opportunities have led to world-wide travel and inevitably to the sampling of different foods, changed habits and customs. Some people formed an antipathy to animal-based products, ushering in vegetarian diets, which previously had been regarded as fare for food freaks. What was a slow undercurrent swelled into a swiftly running stream of fresh ideas, reinforced by increasing anxiety concerning high cholesterol levels in Western foods.

"You are what you eat," trumpeted the Government in the sixties and seventies, appalled at so many overweight children and the clogged-up arteries of parents. Personalities like Roy Castle joined the fitness campaign. Fresh from abroad, young people wooed flavour and variety: pizzas; lasagne; noodles; yoghurt; goat's cheese; curry; moussaka. On the High Street, Chinese, Thai, Indian, Greek and Italian restaurants were eager and ready to oblige. Even the time-honoured fish and chip shop had to cater for new tastes, but it is worth remembering that the industrial towns of Lancashire, once ringed with mills, inherited that godsend, the take-away tradition. In Leigh, up to the 1930s, a man with a sturdy box mounted on his tricycle delivered juicy meat and fruit pies. Cooked meat shops made black puddings – perhaps the oldest is Chadwick's of Waterfoot who have "stood" Bury Market for years. Savoury ducks were dreamed up from pigs' livers, breadcrumbs and herbs; hot peas and gravy could be had to fill a basin. There were roasted potatoes, jacket potatoes, tripe in variety and even hot udder on certain nights.

In the new millennium, eating out, wining and dining have become essential accompaniments to the good life but there is nothing pleasanter than relaxing over "that meal with a difference" in good company, and there is much to be said for producing interesting food at home. Both nostalgia and taste buds dictate that the intriguing charms of old recipes are not lost. Easter spiced biscuits have come down to us from the Anglo-Saxon *Eastre*, dawn-goddess of Springtime. Wet Nellie, based on Madeira cake soaked in Madeira wine, was enjoyed by no less than Lord Nelson. History abounds in recipes. Let it not be lost in the mists of time.

The storm, if not the anxiety, over beef and eggs may be subsiding but the cry goes up "Organic" and will not go away. Kent is working hard to become the organic garden of England, so why should Lancashire not be the organic vegetable garden of England? We have the finest on earth, as indeed English food itself was once the envy of the world. There was fresh fish from cleaner seas and rivers, vegetables from loamy, chemical-free soils, birds and animals that roved free and wild fruits freshly picked.

The Lancashire chefs we have met are passionate about preparation, freshness and the possibilities offered by such a range of choice. They point out that only from quality can come the best results. Their cooking is frequently traditionally based with local ingredients bought fresh daily. Flavour comes from freshly chopped herbs rather than salt. Puddings are hearty, cheeseboards excellently varied, wines well chosen.

To reduce concern about cholesterol, in the following recipes vegetable fat may be substituted for lard or dripping although the flavour will not be quite the same. Because our ancestors walked miles and often worked in the open air, the cholesterol menace was not so great. The car-bound may need to avoid butter, cream and sugar, but the young, with their work-outs and jogging, can have a more light-hearted approach.

Whether you are young or old, good food in moderation remains one of the joys of life and interest in it grows yearly. In May 1999, a leather-bound 15th-century cookery book written in Latin was sold at auction for £10,000. Thought to be the oldest in existence, it contained such recipes as "bear cooked on the bone" and "hare with asparagus"!

By the way, in old Lancashire one never said "bon appétit". I was told that my smiling paternal grandfather, erstwhile landlord of the Dog Inn at Yate and Pickup Bank near Blackburn, when surveying a groaning table, would roar "Friends and neighbours, you are welcome. Reach to."

Catherine Rothwell

Contents

To Eddie
– my beloved husband

Introduction

Throughout this book:

- All recipes serve four people unless otherwise stated
- Eggs are medium size
- Imperial and metric measures are included – use one or the other, but do not mix them.
- Oven temperatures and cooking times are intended as a guide. If using a fan-oven, reduce temperatures by 20 degrees Fahrenheit.

Imperial Weights and Measures with Recommended Metric Equivalents

Ounces	Grams		Pints	Fluid Ounces	Millilitres
1	25		¼ pint	5	150
2	50		½ pint	10	300
3	75		¾ pint	15	450
4	110		1 pint	20	600
5	150		1½ pints	30	900
6	175		1¾ pints	35	1000 (1 litre)
7	200				
8	225				
9	250				
10	275				
11	300				
12	350				
13	375				
14	400				
15	425				
16 (1 lb)	450				

1 cup flour = 4 oz = 110 g
1 cup sugar = 6 oz = 175 g
1 cup butter = 8 oz = 225 g

Oven Temperatures

	C	F	Gas Mark
Very Cool	110	225	¼
	120	250	½
Cool	140	275	1
	150	300	2
Moderate	160	325	3
	180	350	4
Moderately Hot	190	375	5
	200	400	6
Hot	220	425	7
	230	450	8
Very Hot	240	475	9

Start the Day!

Oat Bran Porridge

For this very basic porridge, use ½ pint (300 ml) of cold water to 3 tablespoons of oat bran. Stir and bring gradually to the boil. Cook for 5 minutes to thicken. Serve with milk, sugar and whatever takes your fancy.

Oatmeal Porridge

The Roman Legions depended upon this ancient standby, which is again becoming popular as part of a healthy diet. No longer is it "Go to work on an egg", but "go to work on porridge" as it is low in sodium and fat, thus protecting against heart disease and stabilising blood levels, it is a good source of calcium, iron and vitamin Bl and is easily assimilated.

---

8 fl oz (250 ml) full cream milk or water
2 heaped tablespoons of pinhead oatmeal
a pinch of salt

Pour the cold milk over the oatmeal and leave covered overnight to soak. It will soften and swell. In the morning transfer to a pan and heat slowly, stirring with a wooden spoon until the porridge boils. Add runny honey or sugar if desired and double cream, but that is optional.

Sausages with fried bread

---

1 lb (450 g), sausages
1 oz (25 g) beef dripping
6 small slices bread

Melt the dripping in a heavy frying pan. Prick the sausages and place in the pan, cooking slowly for 20 minutes and turning them several times but not browning them too much until they are cooked through.

Keep the sausages hot in a dish and and put the pieces of bread in the hot dripping. Increase the heat and fry until the bread is crisp. Place each sausage on a piece of fried bread and serve very hot.

23-year-old Robert E Sykes of Pilling won the Gold Award for traditional pork sausages and speciality Cumberland sausages at his first entry for the British Meat Awards at Haydock Park in 1999. Robert took over the Carleton butcher's shop when Jim Watson retired. Jim's Rack of Lamb is featured on page 37.

Grilled Kidneys, bacon and tomatoes

4 sheep's kidneys
½ oz (10 g) butter
4 thin rashers of bacon
2 large tomatoes
salt and pepper

Skin kidneys and cut them almost through. Brush over with virgin olive oil or butter and dredge on salt and pepper.

Put, cut sides up, under the grill. After three minutes, place the thin rashers of bacon around the kidneys, then the tomatoes, halved. Cook for five minutes, turning only once and serve very hot.

In Victorian times this was served at breakfast with Gentleman's Relish.

Fluffy scrambled egg

4 slices buttered toast
4 free range eggs
½ cup of milk
1 spoonful Herbes de Provence
2 oz (50 g) Lancashire cheese, crumbled
nut of butter

In a double saucepan containing the nut of butter, cook the well-whipped eggs with the cheese, milk and herbs gently until they rise, set and fluffy. Use at once, having slices of buttered toast ready. It takes 3-4 minutes, no more, or the texture of the egg will be ruined.

A double saucepan is also invaluable for making Oatmeal Porridge and Lemon Cheese.

Note: Herbes de Provence are frequently used throughout this book – they are a blend of thyme, basil, savory, fennel and lavender)

Kedgeree

10 oz (275 g) long grain brown rice
1½ lbs (675 g) smoked haddock
1 sliced onion
1 bay leaf
2 green peppers
4 tablespoons olive oil
1 thinly sliced large onion
2 oz (50 g) sultanas
2 tablespoons curry power
¼ pint (150 ml) soured cream
ground pepper

Cook the rice in boiling water for 45 minutes until tender. Drain. Run cold water through it and drain. Place the haddock in a saucepan with ground pepper, bay leaf and onion slice. Cover with cold water and simmer for 5 minutes. Lift out the fish, flake it and remove the core and seeds from the peppers and cut them into thin strips. In a large frying pan heat the olive oil on low heat and place in the peppers and thinly sliced onions which should be cooked until soft. Mix in the fish sultanas and curry powder and stir all well together on gentle heat for 5 minutes to bring out the flavours. The soured cream is spread around the edges of the serving dish.

Soups

Carrot Soup

---

1 oz (25 g) butter
8 oz (225 g) grated carrots
1 medium onion grated
1 large potato, peeled and grated
1 pint (600ml) water
1 pint(600ml) milk
1 oz (25 g) rice
pinch of ground nutmeg
2 teaspoons lemon juice
3 tablespoons fresh single cream
ground sea salt and black pepper to taste

Melt the butter and fry the vegetables for 5 minutes. Add the water, milk, rice, nutmeg and seasoning. Bring to the boil, cover and simmer gently for 35 minutes. Stir in the lemon juice and cream.

Lentil and Carrot Soup from Childwall

With any soup, especially Cream of Vegetable, chef John Tovey recommends "a glass of your favourite sherry".

---

7 oz (200 g) lentils
2 large onions
2 large carrots
2 cans chopped tomatoes
1¼ pints (750 ml) stock made from 2 vegetable stock cubes
seasoning

Sauté the sliced onion and chopped carrot and add all the other ingredients to the pan. Simmer for 30 minutes. Ensure that the lentils are soft as lentils should always be well-cooked. Whisk to a soft consistency. Serve piping hot with garlic bread.

Around 1910 the cook on board the *TSS Duke of York*, standing second from the left, served carrot and potato soup as a warmer for passengers and crew on the rough Irish Sea. Other members of the crew are Mr. Piper, Mr. A. Carden, Mr. Wilks, Hornby Leadbetter, the cabin boy, and Mrs. McCaffery, the stewardess. This Lancashire and Yorkshire Railway Company ship, launched in February 1894, sailed on the Belfast to Lancashire run until 1911 when she was sold to Turkey, but the service was discontinued in 1928. From the early 19th century Ireland supplied Lancashire with boxes of butter and eggs, firkins of lard, sacks of wheat and meal, bales of bacon, cattle, horses, fowl, fish and geese. It was an important and friendly trade.

Potato and Watercress Soup

1 oz (25 g) margarine
2 oz (50 g) white part of leek
2 pints (1200 ml) white stock
2 oz (50 g) onion
1 lb (450 g) peeled potatoes
bouquet garni
chopped parsley
small bunch of watercress
salt and pepper

Choose 12 perfect leaves of watercress. Put them in a pan of boiling water for 2 seconds, then immediately refresh them under cold water. These leaves are to garnish the finished soup.

Melt the margarine in a pan and add the sliced onion and leek. Cook for a few minutes without colouring. Add the stock and sliced washed potatoes, bouquet garni, seasoning and the remainder of the watercress including stalks. Simmer for about 30 minutes then remove the bouquet garni. Pass the soup through a sieve, return it to a clean pan, re-boil and correct the seasoning. Sprinkle on a little chopped parsley and add the watercress leaves. Any left over can be kept in the fridge and warmed next day.

Quick Tomato Soup

1 tablespoon sunflower oil
1 medium onion peeled and chopped
1 medium tin tomatoes
1 stock cube
salt and freshly ground black pepper
1 tablespoon chopped parsley

Fry the onion gently in the oil for 3 minutes. Blend the tomatoes and cooked onion in a liquidiser. Pour into a pan and add sufficient water and the prepared stock cube to provide 4 portions of soup. Heat until the soup reaches boiling point then simmer on for 3 minutes. Season to taste. Add the chopped parsley and serve with croutons.

Rossendale Vegetable Broth

Some folk from the Rossendale Valley sprinkle the broth with grated Lancashire cheese immediately prior to serving, but this is optional. *Note: the pulses are to be soaked overnight.*

8 oz (225 g) mixed pulses: yellow split peas and pearl barley
and red lentils, soaked overnight
6 oz (175 g) carrots, peeled and diced
6 oz (175 g) swede peeled and diced
4 peeled and chopped tomatoes (remove the skins by pouring
boiling water over them)
6 oz (175 g) onion peeled and chopped
2½ pints (1½ litres) water
1 vegetable stock cube
1 bay leaf
freshly ground black pepper

Soak the pulses overnight in a bowl covered with cold water. Next morning drain off the liquid, cover the pulses with water and boil for 10 minutes, then skim. Add the tomatoes, carrots, swede and onion to the pan along with the water, crumbled stock cube and bay leaf. Bring to the boil, then reduce to a simmer for 45 minutes. Season to taste.

Dumplings, to add to the Broth

½ teaspoon baking powder

2 oz (50 g) porridge oats

¼ teaspoon dried thyme

4 oz (110 g) self raising flour

2 tablespoon fresh chopped parsley

ground sea salt and black peppercorns

5 tablespoons water

Place the flour, baking powder and oats in a bowl with the thyme, parsley and seasoning. With a little water mix into a soft dough, but not sticky. On a floured board form the dough into small dumplings. Place them on the surface of the **Rossendale Broth**, adding a little more liquid if necessary. Simmer for another 30 minutes to cook them through.

Salford Pea and Ham Soup

1 oz (25 g) soft margarine

1 medium onion peeled and chopped

¾ pint (450 ml) water

12 oz (350 g) thawed out frozen peas

1 stock cube

2 thick slices cooked ham chopped finely with the fat removed

freshly ground black pepper

Fry the onion in the margarine until it is soft and transparent. Put into the pan half of the water, the peas and the melted stock cube. Bring to the boil, then simmer for 10 minutes. Add the rest of the water and liquidise. Put back into the pan and add the ham. Heat gently and simmer on for 2 minutes, stirring all the time. Add the ground pepper last and serve with strips of warm toast.

BLACKBURN CATHEDRAL.

Blackburn Cathedral 1942, before the Lantern was built: sunlight filtering through the eight beautiful new stained glass windows designed by Linda Walton for the restored lantern tower of Blackburn Cathedral casts a glorious pattern of colours on walls and organ, reminiscent of lines from John Keats' poem, "The Eve of St. Agnes" – "Innumerable stains and splendid dyes, rose bloom, soft amethyst ..."

Leek and Potato Soup

Cathedral catering is frequently very good. Liverpool Anglican Cathedral enjoyed a reputation for the best fish and chips when we last visited. Truro Cathedral found that its lemon meringue pie and fairy cakes were best sellers. And, soup of the day at Blackburn Cathedral's "Cafe in the Crypt" was leek and potato soup – so here's my recipe to remind me of that brilliant, crisp day in March 1999:

---

8 oz (225 g) leeks
1 oz (25 g) butter
1 teaspoon wholemeal flour
2 peeled medium-sized potatoes
2 teaspoons whole grain mustard
1¼ pints (750 ml) stock
¼ pint (150 ml) dry white wine
3 tablespoons chopped parsley

Finely chop the potatoes and leeks. Melt the butter on a low heat and stir in the chopped vegetables. Cover and allow to sweat in the butter for 5 minutes. Stir in the flour, mustard and stock and bring to the boil, stirring all the time. Simmer uncovered for 20 minutes then add the wine and parsley. Re-heat gently but do not boil.

Cauliflower and Almond Soup

This recipe was supplied by the staff from the kitchen at Alston Hall Residential College, Longridge.

---

1 medium cauliflower

1 medium onion

2 tablespoons oil

7½ oz (210 g) can of tomatoes

2 oz (50 g) almonds

1 pint (600 ml) chicken stock

¼ pint (150 ml) milk

1 oz (25 g) wholemeal flour

¼ pint (150 ml) single cream

½ teaspoon chilli powder

salt and pepper to taste

Wash and trim the cauliflower and break into florets. Bring a large pan of water to the boil and add the cauliflower. Simmer for 5 minutes then drain. Peel and slice the onion. Heat the oil in a pan. Add the onion and fry for 3 minutes. Add the tomatoes, almonds, cauliflower, chicken stock, milk and flour. Stir well. Bring to the boil then reduce the heat and simmer for 10 minutes. Place the soup into a blender and run until a smooth consistency is achieved. Return to the pan, stir in the cream over gentle heat but do not boil. Season with the chilli powder, salt and pepper. Serve piping hot with croutons and a sprinkling of chopped fresh parsley.

Blackstone Edge on the Pennine Way, "noted all over England for a dismal high precipice" (Celia Fiennes 1662-1741), drew travellers to the Coach and Horses Inn. This ancient inn, also known as Ye Olde White Horse, 1,300 feet above sea level, had James Palmer as proprietor in 1920, who catered for cyclists and walkers with hot soup, sandwiches, coffee and a blazing peat fire.

This team of 4 men and 6 ladies is thought to have worked at a cannery in Liverpool about 1930 at a time when hygiene was becoming more important. White overalls and caps were demanded by factory inspectors. Reckitts advertised: "Out of the blue comes the whitest wash". It was the "dolly blue" in the final rinse that produced the whitest of overalls.

Winter Broth

1 lb (450 g) washed, diced vegetables (carrots, turnips, leeks)

4 oz (110 g) shredded cabbage

1 bay leaf

1 pint (600 ml) vegetable stock

1 teaspoon mango chutney

1½ pints (900 ml) boiling water

1 oz (25 g) rolled oats

Simmer the chopped vegetables in the stock with the bay leaf for 20 minutes.

Add the cabbage, chutney and oats and simmer for a further 15 minutes then remove the bay leaf. Serve very hot with buttered toast "soldiers".

Onion Soup

This recipe was given to me by a Spanish chef on board the P & O cruise liner *Sea Princess*. He also taught me how to peel and cook onions: before peeling, cut the onion in half from top to bottom. Yank back the skin from each half and lop off the root. The slow sweating in oil and butter sweetens and improves flavour. As for chicken stock, although stock cubes are fine, the real thing is better.

---

1 oz (25 g) butter
4 large Spanish onions
1 dessertspoon sunflower oil
4 slices of old bread, dried crisply
2 pints (1200 ml) chicken stock
sprig of fresh sage or thyme well-chopped

Melt the butter in the oil. Slice the onions thinly and "sweat" them over low heat. Cover the pan for 35 minutes, stirring occasionally. Add the sage or thyme. Put in the stock and bring to the boil for 3 minutes. Add a layer of bread to each serving and finish with grated cheese.

Chicken Stock

A few days before you make the stock, collect the washed outer leaves of lettuce, skins of onions, clean peelings and rough outer stems of root vegetables. Keep them in a plastic bag in the fridge ready for the stockpot. Place these round the chicken carcass in a deep pan and cover with cold water. Simmer for as long as possible, adding water, but never allowing to boil. Sieve and use within a day or two.

Snacks & Savouries

Bubble and Squeak

The name of this dish is said to derive from the sounds it makes while cooking!

---

2 oz (50 g) lard or 1 oz beef dripping
seasoning
the leftovers from mashed potatoes (about 8 oz) and
well-chopped cooked cabbage (about 4 oz)

Mix the potatoes and cabbage well together and season as desired. Melt the lard in a frying pan and smooth in the potato and cabbage mixture. Press down, making a round "cake" shape. Fry on both sides until all is nicely browned and firm. In old Lancashire, especially Blackburn, they used real beef dripping. Cheap, quick and tasty.

Bowland Spaghetti/Pasta Bake

This recipe came from a friend during World War II when food was rationed and all sorts of ingenious ideas prevailed. He used spaghetti but pasta might be more popular now – hence the title. I preferred to place the mixture in a Pyrex dish covered only with a pastry crust as the stock tended to make a pastry base soggy.

---

4 oz (110 g) spaghetti/pasta
8 oz (225 g) cold pheasant
¼ pint (150 ml) stock
2 oz (50 g) grated cheese
8 oz (225 g) thinly rolled shortcrust pastry (or half this amount
if you only make a pastry lid)
a little cream

Break the spaghetti into pieces 2 ins (5 cm) long. Boil in salted water for 20 minutes. Allow to cool. Cut the pheasant into small pieces but do not mince. Line a cake tin with very thin pastry and fill with layers of pheasant, spaghetti and cheese. Moisten well with the stock and cream and cover with a thin pastry lid. Bake for 30 minutes in a hot oven.

Pendle Forest under snow. In the winter of 1851 farmer John Parkinson, too old and infirm to work any longer at Paradise Farm, looks back sadly at his old home. His son Henry took him to live at Accrington.

Lentil Mould with Boiled Bacon

½ pint (300 ml) red split lentils
1½ oz (40 g) butter
1 tablespoon cornflour
1 onion
½ a cupful milk
2 eggs

Allow the lentils to soak overnight. Wash them. Peel the onion and cut into quarters. Put both in a saucepan with about ¾ pint (450 ml) boiling water. Simmer until soft, not adding salt until then. Rub the well-cooked lentils through a sieve and keep the lentil water for soup. Melt the butter and add the lentil purée. Mix the cornflour into the milk and beat the eggs. Pour the milk and cornflour onto the eggs, adding gradually to the purée. Grease a pie dish, pour in the mixture and bake for 30 minutes till set. The lentil mould can be turned out and served with croutons and boiled bacon. This is an old Lancashire sustaining meal full of protein for manual workers.

Veal Loaf

1 oz (25 g) butter, fresh from the fridge, roughly chopped
8 oz (225 g) lightly cooked cold veal
2 eggs
1 cupful fresh breadcrumbs
4 rashers bacon
2 tablespoons hot milk
grated peel of 1 lemon
1 tablespoon dried breadcrumbs
salt and pepper

Soak the fresh breadcrumbs in the hot milk and squeeze out. Mince the meat and *unsoftened* butter and add to the breadcrumbs with the grated lemon peel and seasoning. Beat the eggs and add to the mixture. Shape the veal loaf, retaining a little egg to brush over the loaf which should be rolled in dried breadcrumbs. Place in a baking tin and bake in a hot oven until nicely browned. After 20 minutes roll up the rashers of bacon and place these on top of the loaf. When the bacon rolls also have cooked, serve the loaf with slices of freshly cut ripe tomatoes.

Cheese and Bacon Omelette

This is tasty with pickled samphire, but unpolluted samphire is growing increasingly rare. A Southport octogenarian told me it can still be found on the salt marshes of Lancashire. Country folk who had no other source of income used to gather samphire and sell it in the villages.

---

12 oz (350 g) potatoes

3 tablespoons olive oil

3 crushed garlic cloves

6 oz (175 g) lean bacon cut into strips

6 free range eggs

1 onion peeled and sliced

4 oz (110 g) grated Lancashire cheese

2 tablespoons chopped parsley

freshly ground salt and black pepper

Cook the diced potatoes for 15 minutes, then drain. Heat the oil and fry the onion and garlic for 4 minutes. Add the potatoes and bacon and cook on for a few minutes until the onion has softened. With 2 tablespoons of milk and 2 of water beat the eggs lightly and add the chopped parsley and seasoning. Pour into the pan and sprinkle with the grated cheese. Keep the mixture moving, stroking it with a fork from the edge of the pan. It will begin to set after a few minutes. Do not overcook. Five minutes should be adequate.

If you can find fresh samphire, first wash it well to remove any sand. Spread it on a cloth to dry in the sun and fresh air. Put it in a pan with enough malt vinegar to cover the samphire and add 1 teaspoon of ground ginger. Allow it to boil until it changes colour and will easily slip off the stalks. Put it into jars and cover with malt vinegar.

O'Brien Potatoes

The recipe for these deliciously different potatoes was sent by cookery tutor Glynis Best who prefers the small, waxy type of potatoes which hold their shape, although most varieties are suitable. As this makes a large quantity it should go down well at Harvest Suppers with sliced beef or boiled chicken, a change from hot pot and pickled red cabbage.

1 large diced onion
3 lbs (1.5 kg) peeled, diced potatoes
2 cloves of crushed garlic
2 oz (50 g) mixed diced peppers
½ teaspoon chilli powder
1 level teaspoon paprika
1 level tablespoon parmesan cheese
1 pint (600 ml) single or double cream
¼ pint (150 ml) milk
a little salt and pepper

Place the diced potatoes in a deep, oven-proof casserole dish, add the onions, peppers, garlic, seasoning and cheese and mix well. In a separate jug mix the cream and milk together and cover the potato with this mixture. Place in a pre-heated oven at 200 C (400 F) for 20 minutes, then reduce the temperature to 190 C (375 F) and cook on for a further 40 minutes.

Fish

Fishing Smacks at Jubilee Quay, Fleetwood: Fleetwood was once the third most important fishing port in England and the premier hake port. In 1919 a harvest of £1,500,000 was reaped from the sea and most of the townspeople were involved in the fishing industry. Associated trades included net braiding, box making, ships' chandlers, rope making, boat building, trawlers' supplies, ice factory and smokehouses. Fleetwood was indeed a household name for top quality white fish. There were shrimps, prawns, mussels, cockles and herrings in abundance, all much relied upon by Lancashire housewives for cheap, nourishing recipes.

A Good Fish Stock

2 lbs (900 g) of fish bones and trimmings
6 white peppercorns
1 large Spanish onion
1 large tomato
2 pints (1200 ml) water
½ teaspoon coarse salt
½ blade mace
1 bay leaf
1 small carrot

A "hotch potch" of shrimp shells and lobster shells can form the basis, but not mackerel or salmon trimmings as these are oily. Wash the vegetables and chop them up small. Cut the trimmings up small. Tie up the herbs and spices in muslin. Put the ingredients into a stew pan, bring to the boil, then simmer for ¾ hour. Make sure the stock is strained carefully to eliminate any fish bones. Use it straight away as fish stock should always be freshly made.

Potted Buttered Shrimps

If possible, use freshly caught shrimps boiled aboard the shrimper or "nobby".

2 pint (600 ml) cans of fresh, boiled, peeled shrimps
4 oz (110 g) best butter
pepper and salt
¼ teaspoon of powdered mace

Soften the butter. Mix the indredients well, then press the mixture into pots and leave until the butter is set. Pour over another 2 oz (50 g) of melted butter and leave to cool. Garnish with lemon and parsley,

Few sailors learned to swim because they were too superstitious, so when his shrimper "Judy" sank near Nelson Buoy, "Couch" Wright simply climbed onto the buoy and waited to be picked up by a passing trawler. Undeterred, he acquired another shrimper, "Charlotte". A distinguished lifeboatman, he carried exhausted Belgian sailors from the steam trawler "Commandant Bultinck" which was wrecked off Rossall School in 1929.

Lytham Shrimps Clifton

This recipe, supplied by John Gledhill when Head Chef at the Clifton Arms, Lytham, makes four portions.

12 oz (350 g) peeled shrimps
2 oz (50 g) butter
1 clove of garlic
¼ pint (150 ml) double cream
1 teaspoon brandy
2 oz (50 g) parsley
ground black peppercorns
sippets (about 1" squares) of toast
ground sea salt

Melt the butter in a small saucepan and add the finely chopped garlic. Add the shrimps to the butter and garlic, stirring constantly for 30 seconds. Add the brandy, flambé and pour in the cream. Simmer for 2 minutes. Season with the peppercorns and salt. Scatter on the sippets and sprigs of parsley.

At Southport Potted Shrimps, 66 Station Road, Banks Village, Southport, the Peel family, who have been involved in the local brown shrimp industry for four generations, use a unique blend of herbs and butter in their traditional processing.

Plaice Velouté

Velouté is a rich, velvety sauce. It adds a touch of luxury to this fish dish:

4 large plaice fillets
1 tablespoon cooking oil
2 tomatoes skinned and chopped
1 small finely chopped onion
6 oz (175 g) peeled prawns
2 oz (50 g) white breadcrumbs
ground white pepper
2 oz (50 g) butter
2 oz (50 g) plain flour
1 pint (600 ml) milk
5 tablespoons single cream
½ teaspoon powdered dill
Salt

Wash and skin the fish. Heat the oil and gently fry the onion until soft. Add the skinned and chopped tomatoes and peeled prawns and cook for 2 minutes. Stir in the breadcrumbs. Season with salt and pepper. Spread over the plaice fillets and keep them warm in an ovenproof dish.

Melt the batter in a pan. Stir in the flour and cook over low heat for 2 minutes, then gradually blend in the milk and bring to the boil. Add the powdered dill, cream and salt. Stir it well and pour over the fish in the oven-proof dish. Cook in the oven for 20 minutes at 190 C, 375 F.

Grilled Hake

4 cutlets or slices of hake about 5 oz (150 g) each
2 oz (50 g) melted butter
1 tablespoon of lemon juice
seasoning (salt and ground peppercorns)

Coat the slices of hake in melted butter and scatter on seasoning to taste. Pour lemon juice over the fish and place under a hot grill, but not too close. After 7 minutes turn the pieces over and grill the other side for 7 minutes. Around the turn of the 19th century, hake, known in Fleetwood as "black mouths", was so despised it was thrown back into the sea until smacksman Sam Colley tried a 'molly hamperful' (in the 1940s, this was the term for a basket of fish) on a Manchester market. It was so popular that, from then on, demand for hake grew rapidly. Silver hake was also to become scarce, yet at one time supplies were so plentiful, fish was given away to needy families.

Soused Herrings

Kipper, derived from herring, was the poor man's smoked salmon. Soaked overnight in lemon juice, it needed no further cooking. With the liquid drained off all bones removed, it was mashed up with a little butter and spread on brown bread. Sadly, as with hake, the shoals of herring vanished in the late 1920s.

6 herrings
1 medium-sized onion
3 bay leaves
6 peppercorns
sea salt and black pepper
parsley
vinegar and water

Clean scrape and bone the fresh herrings. Slit open and lay them flat on a

The Maude Pickup Lifeboat and Crew: Trawlermen faced great hazards whilst deep sea fishing. On June 16th 1897, the Maude Pickup made history by rescuing 18 men from three wrecked ships. In the picture are Thomas, Jack, William and David Leadbetter, "Judy" and Toby Wright, Jim Roskell, John Salthouse, Charlie Hughes, Matt Boardman, F. Bettess, Max Cowell, Billy Croft, and Coxwain Billy Wright. The main occupation of these brave men was fishing in the coastal waters and the deep seas.

board. Place two slices of onion with seasoning upon each and roll them up, starting at the head. Pack them tightly together in an oven-proof dish, placing half a bay leaf between each two fish. Cover with one part vinegar, one part water and add the peppercorns and chopped parsley. Bake for an hour in a moderate oven.

Boiled Mackerel with Horseradish Sauce

During the 18th and 19th centuries, horseradish was as widely used in fish dishes as we now use parsley. Years ago when almost every humble cottage had land attached for fruit bushes and apple trees, gooseberry sauce was a favourite with mackerel to cut the oiliness.

---

6 small mackerel
½ teaspoon mace
2 tablespoons white vinegar
1 teaspoon butter
4 anchovies
1 teaspoon flour
juice of 2 lemons
1 teaspoon horseradish sauce
salt and pepper

Put the mackerel in a pan, add the vinegar, sprinkle the mace and cover with water. Bring to the boil then simmer gently for 15 minutes. During this time chop the anchovies fine and mix with the lemon juice in another pan. Once the fish are cooked, add 1 pint (600 ml) of the cooking water into the second pan, bring to the boil and simmer for five minutes. Bone the fish and lay them in a serving dish, cover and keep warm. Mix the softened butter and flour with the horseradish sauce and add a little water. Cook on for two minutes until the sauce has thickened slightly, then spoon it over the fish in the serving dish. Serve with rice or boiled new potatoes.

Gooseberry Sauce

This is the sauce mentioned above as being ideal to serve with mackerel – or with any other oily fish.

1 lb (450 g) green gooseberries
6 tablespoons sugar
1 oz (25 g) butter
¼ pint (150 ml) water
parsley
seasoning

Place all the ingredients, except the parsley, in a pan and simmer until the gooseberries are tender. Pour over the cooked mackerel and garnish with well-chopped parsley.

Haddock with Egg Sauce

Haddock tastes best from October to January before the February-March spawning begins.

4 slices haddock
2 tablespoons butter
½ pint (300 ml) milk
3 hard-boiled eggs
1 small onion
flour
seasoning

Cook the fish for 15 minutes in gently boiling water which has had a little malt vinegar and seasoning added. Whilst this is cooking make the egg sauce by melting 2 tablespoons of butter in 1 tablespoon of flour. Stir in the milk that has been gently simmered, with the small, peeled onion. As the sauce thickens add the finely chopped whites of the 3 hard-boiled eggs and lastly the finely sieved egg yolks.

Trawlerman's Pie

---

2 lbs (900 g) cod
2 lbs (900 g) mashed floury potatoes
6 oz (175 g) mushrooms
2 oz (50 g) butter
1 pint (600 ml) milk

Wash the fish. Wash, slice and gently cook the mushrooms in a frying pan with 1 oz (25 g) of butter. Poach the cod, adding a little malt vinegar or lemon to the liquid. Flake the fish well, being careful to remove any bones and skin. Around the edges of the large oven-proof dish place the mashed potato and, in the centre, put the flaked fish. Scatter a little milk over the fish and potatoes, then add the mushrooms. Cover with white sauce made from the rest of the milk, 1 oz (25 g) of cornflour and a tablespoon of chopped parsely. Bake for 30 minutes in a moderate oven.

Salamgundi

Brown bread and butter tastes good with Salamgundi, an old Lancashire recipe known as Salomongundy in the 18th century when anchovies were considered an essential ingredient. This version of the old recipe was kindly supplied by the Moorcock Inn near Waddington.

---

8 oz (225 g) sliced, smoked salmon
chopped parsley
2 oz (50 g melted butter
lemon juice
ground black pepper
ground sea salt to taste

Lay 4 oz (110 g) of the salmon flat on greased, greaseproof paper to form a rectangle. Put the rest of the smoked salmon and all other ingredients into a blender until a smooth paste is formed. Season and place this mixture into the centre of your rectangle. Roll tightly and refrigerate for 12 hours, by which time it will be firm. Slice with a hot knife and serve garnished with cucumber, watercress and parsley.

Sea Food Fantasy

Garnished with parsley and whole cooked prawns in their shells, this dish looks professional – not surprisingly, as this recipe was supplied by Ian M.T. Carter, former chef at the Clifton Arms Hotel, Lytham.

---

2 oz (50 g) butter

4 oz (110 g) prawns

4 oz (110 g) diced halibut

4 oz (110 g) salmon tail

½ oz (15 g) mild curry powder

2 oz (50 g) finely chopped onion

½ diced red pepper

½ diced fresh pineapple

1 teaspoon mango chutney

¼ pint (150 ml) double cream

sea salt

ground black pepper

Melt the butter in a medium sized saucepan. Add the onion and curry powder. Cook for one minute only; do not brown. Add the red pepper and pineapple and cook on for a further two minutes. Add the halibut and salmon and give it another two minutes. Pour in the double cream, mango chutney and prawns and simmer gently for five minutes. Serve with rice and a scattering of black pepper and sea salt.

Seafood Crumble

Chef Carl Sims was providing main courses for 100 boys when we last called at the renowned Stoneyhurst College in the Ribble Valley. His recipe for Seafood Crumble uses 10 lbs cod, 4 lbs prawns, 4 lbs mussels and 2 lbs cockles plus three gallons of fish velouté (see page 21), breadcrumbs, Cheddar cheese and lemon. I dare not attempt to reduce this banquet to a table for two. We wished we could have stayed for dinner!

Salmon Pie

½ lb (225 g) fresh salmon (tail piece)
1 sliced lemon
2 cups white wine
2 cups water
6 oz (175 g) white flour
salt, pepper and banquet garni
6 oz (175 g) wholemeal flour
8 chopped anchovies
2 oz (50 g) soft butter
2 oz (50 g) brown breadcrumbs
5 oz (150 g) butter
2 teaspoons mixed herbs
extra seasoning and oil

Along with water, wine, seasoning and bouquet garni bring the salmon to the boil in a pan then simmer for 15 minutes. Make the pastry by rubbing the 5 oz (150 g) butter into the two kinds of flour mixed together. Bind by adding enough cold water to make stiff dough.

Roll out two thirds of the pastry and with it line a loose-bottomed 9 inch (23 cm) cake tin. Mix together the chopped anchovies, soft butter, breadcrumbs, herbs and seasoning, blending all with a tablespoon of olive oil or the oil from the anchovies. Form into balls. Fill the pie tin with salmon pieces intermingled with the balls. With the remaining pastry make a lid for the pie, leaving a hole in the centre. Bake in a moderate oven for 35 minutes and half way through, pour half a cup of the cooking juices through the hole in the pastry lid. Good with salad.

Salmon Scallops

1 medium tin of salmon
1 oz (25 g) butter
1 oz (25 g) flour
½ pint (300 ml) milk
1 teaspoon lemon juice
4 oz (110 g) grated Cheddar cheese

Grease 6 scallop shells. Make a roux sauce with the butter, flour and milk. Add

Glasson Dock

lemon juice, stir in half of the grated cheese and cook gently. Stir in the salmon. Put this mixture in the shells and sprinkle the rest of the grated cheese on top. Brown under the grill.

Salmon Loaf

1 medium tin of salmon
3 fl oz (90 ml) milk
2 oz (50 g) dried breadcrumbs
2 eggs
1 teaspoon salt
1 teaspoon lemon juice

Take the skin and bone out of the salmon and mash well. Put breadcrumbs into a bowl. Heat the milk and pour it onto the crumbs. Add the salmon to the breadcrumbs plus salt, lemon juice and egg yolks. Mix well together. Whip up egg whites stiffly and fold in. Pour into a well-greased 1 lb (450 g) loaf tin and bake just above the centre of the oven for about ¾ hour at 190 C (375 F). It can be eaten sliced with salad or cucumber. Garnish with lemon wedges and parsley.

The Port of Lancaster Smoked Salmon Co. of West Quay, Glasson Dock is a family firm producing a superior grade of smoked Scottish salmon. It is also well-known for smoked hams, bacon, trout, duck breast, chicken and game.

Baked Trout

Silvery trout, caught in the rivers and streams, are smaller than lake and sea trout, but just as delicious. Bake, grill or fry but do not boil. Cook as soon as possible, sprinkled with lemon, in a buttered ovenproof dish. Cover and bake in a moderate oven for 20 minutes.

2 large or 4 small trout
1 tablespoon of white vinegar
1 small onion
1 tablespoon fresh lemon juice
1 oz (25 g) butter
sprig of thyme
1 teaspoon flour
sea salt

Clean the trout and remove the scales. Put the vinegar, thyme, chopped onion and a sprinkle of ground sea salt with 3 tablespoons of water in a saucepan and simmer for 5 minutes. Strain the liquor into a ovenproof dish. Put in the trout and bake in a moderate oven for 30 minutes. While cooking, baste frequently with the liquor. Place the trout on a hot dish. Sprinkle the flour into the liquor, add the butter and stir until it boils on for 5 minutes. Strain, then add the lemon juice. Make very hot once more and pour it over the fish.

River Trout Poached in Red Wine

Both trout and salmon were once plentiful in Lancashire rivers such as the Lune, Ribble, Wyre, Hodder and Calder. In pre-war days at the Whitewell Hotel, near Clitheroe we enjoyed trout stuffed with butter and garnished with lemon slices. Freshly caught and baked for 20 minutes in a moderate oven, it needed neither sauce nor wine. Here, however, is a recipe with a difference:

1 lb (450 g) fresh trout
1 glass of red wine
2 lemons
1 onion
salt and pepper
water to cover

Thinly slice the onion and peeled lemons with a sharp knife and place on top of the washed trout in a deep pan. Season with salt and pepper. Heat the wine, adding sufficient water to cover the trout. Bring to the boil then gently poach for 15 minutes. Brush with melted butter and serve with lemon slices.

Scalloped Lobster

When lobsters were more plentiful and less expensive than today, this 1883 recipe states:

"Crack up the lobster and simmer in the stock for half an hour. Add some Lancashire Relish, chopped shallot and chopped parsley. Cool. Extract the lobster and array in scollop shells. Sprinkle with breadcrumbs and dot with butter. Place in a moderate oven until lightly browned."

---

1 fresh lobster
breadcrumbs
2 pints (1200 ml) stock
chopped shallot and chopped parsley
pepper, salt, butter

In the 17th century Thomas Jordan (1612-1685) wrote "Fish dinners will make a lass spring like a flea. Have oysters and lobsters to cure melancholy."

Eel with Paprika

---

2 small eels
2 cloves garlic
2 small onions
2 pints (1200 ml) dry white wine
bunch of herbs
½ teaspoon paprika
1 teaspoon salt

Wash and skin the eels and cut into small pieces with the chopped onions, crushed garlic, herbs, salt and paprika. Simmer gently in the wine for half an hour in a pan with a well-fitting lid or pressure cook for 10 minutes.

Hundreds of eels bred in the many ponds throughout the Fylde of Lancashire. These ponds were originally marl pits which filled with water when no longer used for storing clay as a soil conditioner. A long-handled, three-pronged

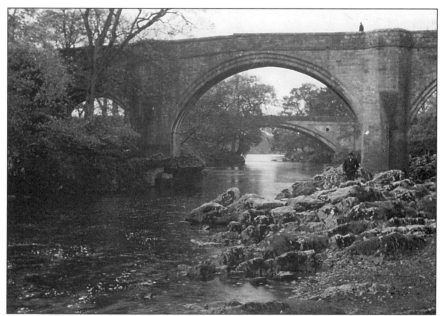

Devil's Bridge, Kirkby Lonsdale, 1904, when this was part of Lancashire and a most beautiful river in which to go fishing.

spear was used to catch the eels, which were collected in bags and either taken home or hawked around the villages and were often made into pies.

Southport Cockle Pie

The pastry for savoury pies was made with butter or beef dripping but this traditional recipe uses lard:

---

1 quart (200 ml) cockles
4 oz (110 g) lard
8 oz (225 g) plain flour
1 large rasher of streaky bacon
a generous dessertspoonful of cold water
a scattering of chopped chives

Rub the flour into the lard, using the tips of the fingers, but avoid overdoing the water or the pastry will be heavy. Have the pastry board lightly floured. Line the sides of a pie dish with this pastry half an inch thick. Cook a quart (1200 ml) of cockles in a cup full of water until the cockles open. Shell the cockles and place a layer of them at the bottom of the dish. Sprinkle them with freshly chopped chives and add a layer of diced, streaky bacon. Add further layers of cockles and bacon until the dish is full. Grind some pepper and over all pour the liquid in which the cockles were cooked. With thin strips of pastry make a lattice-work pattern to cover the top. Gently moisten the strips at each end of the pastry. Cook slowly to ensure the pastry is cooked through and serve hot with new potatoes.

Southport Cockles

Shrimping and cockling off Flookburgh, Southport, Morecambe, Fleetwood and Lytham was once a way of life. The carts set off in convoy and rakes, riddles, baskets and an appliance called "the Jumbo" were used to collect the cockles at low tide,

The tale is told of Billy Birkenhead of Bamber Bridge, a fanatical supporter of Blackburn Rovers, who was mortified when the mighty Rovers were defeated in the F.A. Cup by lowly Southport. After taunts from neighbouring Preston North End Supporters, Billy's indignity was complete when he got up the next morning and found his doorstep swathed in Southport cockle shells.

Meat, Game & Poultry

Kathleen Haslam with two friendly Christmas geese at the Fylde auction Mart where she worked in 1931. Geese were moved to market in flocks along country roads uncluttered with traffic. Their noisy cries were familiar sounds carrying across the fields of the Fylde of Lancashire. In 1897, Christmas geese were reported to be selling for ten pence a pound. Prior to December 25th, "flesh days" were held, when market squares were filled from end to end with stalls of beef, game and poultry. One Lancashire wife took home "a huge ham, a piece of beef, tarts, cheese and a spice cake".

Lancashire Hot Pot

6 middle neck lamb chops
4 lambs' kidneys
8 oz (225 g) sliced onion
2 lbs (900 g) potatoes
8 oz (225 g) carrots
3 oz (75 g) butter
½ pint (300 ml) stock (can be made from a stock cube)
1 teaspoon Herbes de Provence
salt and pepper to taste

Brown the chops in butter after first removing excess fat. Sprinkle the herbs at the bottom of the casserole and stand the chops on end amidst layers of sliced kidneys, carrots and onions. Season and pour the stock over. Top with layers of sliced potatoes brushed with butter. Cover and cook in a moderate oven for 2 hours. Uncover and brown the potatoes for a further 20 minutes.

My mother specified 6 chops because it was for a family of 6. You could use more meat and less potato. She always put strips of bacon over the potatoes in the last 20 minutes of cooking. Don't forget the pickled red cabbage to go with the hot pot!

Liver Hot Pot

1 lb (450 g) lamb's liver
2 oz (50 g) fresh breadcrumbs
salt and pepper
grated nutmeg
1 tablespoon chopped parsley
yolk of 1 egg
8 oz (225 g) back bacon
½ pint (300 ml) stock
4 ripe tomatoes

Slice the liver into 4 portions, wash and pat dry. Mix the breadcrumbs with salt, pepper, nutmeg and parsley and bind with a little egg yolk. Divide the mixture into 4 portions and place I portion on each slice of liver. Wrap each piece of liver in a bacon rasher and place in a greased, oven-proof dish. Pour In the stock. Cook without a lid at 180 C (350 F) for half an hour. Serve with the baked tomatoes, sun-ripened, organic if possible.

Millworker at Enfield Mill, Wigan 1932. "Tatty Pot", the dialect name for Hot Pot, made an excellent meal to come home to after a long day at the local Cotton Spinning Mill. Mothers who worked at the mill left the Hot Pot slowly cooking in the fire oven.

Liverpool Lobscouse

These concise directions are from a true Liverpool fan, the late Harry Hodgkinson:

½ lb (225 g) breast of lamb
3 lbs (1.5 kg) potatoes
1 pint (600 ml) vegetable stock
1 small black pudding chopped up
½ lb (225 g) stewing steak
½ lb (225 g) carrots
½ lb (225 g) parsnips
1 large onion
a good sprinkle of mixed herbs
sea salt and a dash of pepper

Peel the potatoes and vegetables. Wash, trim and cut up the meat. Place all the ingredients together in a stew pot or pan. Bring to the boil and simmer slowly for 2 hours, adding more liquid if required, "but do not drown the scouse".

Steak and Kidney Pudding

A favourite winter dish and an excuse to bring out the pickled red cabbage or the harvest chutney.

---

8 oz (225 g) stewing steak cut into cubes
3 oz (75 g) sliced kidneys
3 oz (75 g) chopped suet
1 chopped onion
8 oz (225 g) plain flour
1 teaspoon baking powder
3 tablespoons water
salt

Mix the flour and suet with the baking powder and ½ teaspoon of salt. Mix to a firm dough with a little cold water. Leave a quarter of the suet pastry to form a lid. Roll out the rest.

Line a greased 1½ pint (900 ml) pudding basin. Combine the kidneys and steak on a board and coat each piece with seasoned flour. Add the chopped onion and put into the pudding basin with 2 tablespoons of water. Roll out the pastry to form a lid that fits the basin and fix it down by damping the edges of the pastry. Cover with two layers of greased greaseproof paper and steam for 4 hours.

Steak and Onions

---

1 lb (450 g) rump steak
2 lbs (900 g) Spanish onions
1 oz (25 g) butter
salt

Peel and thinly slice the onions and put them in a pan of boiling water with ½ teaspoon of salt. After 20 minutes' boiling, strain and place in a frying pan with the butter. Cook gently, stirring frequently. Cut the steak into 4 portions, brush with butter and place under a red-hot grill to brown. Do not pierce the meat with a fork when turning to brown the other Side. Do this quickly to seal in the juices, then grill slowly to make the steak tender, turning about 3 times more and taking about 20 minutes, according to the thickness of the steak.

Keep the onions hot and when the steak is ready, pile them around the meat. The Victorians ate this with Lea and Perrins or Worcester Sauce.

Rack of Lamb

Ask your butcher to prepare in advance a rack of lamb – size depending on how many are to be fed.

Dusted with a garlic and rosemary seasoning and cooked in a moderate oven for 2 hours, this was delicious. Snuggled under the "cave" area where the joint of lamb arches, I put peeled, button mushrooms which emerged perfectly cooked and redolent with the seasoning. Chopped, steamed spring cabbage and sliced potatoes cooked in the oven with the lamb were tasty accompaniments. An enthusiastic butcher like Mr. Jim Watson of The Crescent, Carleton, is an asset. "How about a Crown Roast next weekend?" he said. Mr. Watson recommended glazing the rack of lamb as follows:

½ cupful of honey
½ cupful of brown sugar
½ cupful of orange juice

Mix well. Steaks of game are also improved by this glaze. They can be placed under the grill.

Lamb Steaks

2 lean lamb steaks approx ¾ inch (2 cm) thick
1 sliced tomato
1 dessertspoon fresh basil, chopped
2 oz (50 g) Lancashire Cheese

Wash, pat dry and place the lamb steaks under a pre-heated grill for 6 minutes each side. Half-way through the second cooking, top with tomato, basil and grated cheese. Cook on for 3 minutes. Serve with warm garlic bread and a mixed leaf salad.

Roast lamb is given additional flavour by spiking the joint with sprigs of rosemary after glazing it with apple sauce.

Apple Sauce

2 large Bramley apples
¼ pint (150 ml) cider
1 oz (25 g) butter
2 tablespoons sugar
juice of half a lemon

Peel, core and chop the apples. The cores can be included whole to impart flavour and removed later. Place the apples in a pan with the cider and cook until they "fall" into a pulp but still retain shape, then gently stir in the rest of the ingredients. Serve hot. A favourite also with roast chicken.

Lamb with apricots

Attributed to dramatist John Lyly (1554-1606), "A Serving Man's Song" praises meat above wealth ('coney' = rabbit, and it rhymes with 'money'!):

"O for a plump, fat leg of mutton,

Veal, lamb, capon, pig and coney

None is happy but a glutton,

None an ass but who wants money"

---

1 shoulder of lamb, boned and rolled and well-scattered with chopped, fresh mint

1 large chopped onion

1 tin apricots including the juice

½ pint (300 ml) water

ground sea salt and black pepper

Place all the ingredients in an oblong Pyrex, casserole and cover with foil. Cook until the lamb is tender. Half an hour before serving remove the foil and baste the lamb with the gravy. Serve with roast potatoes and young peas lightly cooked fresh from the pod.

Lamb's Liver with Herbs

---

3 oz (75 g) lamb's liver

1 tablespoon seasoned flour

juice of 1 medium lemon

2 tablespoons extra virgin olive oil

½ teaspoon Herbes de Provence

Slice the liver thinly and coat in the seasoned flour mixed with the herbs. Sprinkle on lemon juice. Fry quickly in the olive oil for 4 minutes, shaking the pan and turning the pieces. Do not overcook.

Pork Pot Roast

About 3 lbs (1.5 kg) boned and rolled leg of pork
8 medium sized onions
8 medium sized potatoes
1 oz (25 g) butter
8 cored, sweet, small apples
¼ pint (150 ml) stock
6 oz (175 g) sage and onion stuffing
chopped parsley
ground salt and pepper

Seal the pork on all sides in a hot, thick pan. Cool and add the butter and brown the sliced onions in it. Add the stock and cover the pan closely. Cook slowly for 1 ½ hours on top of the stove.

Fill the hollow centres of the apples with stuffing and add them to the pan, with the peeled and halved potatoes and seasonings. Continue cooking for another hour until all is tender. Sprinkle chopped parsley over the roast before serving.

Gammon Special

2 lbs (900 g) joint of Danish gammon
2 teaspoons brown sugar
¾ lb (350 g) fresh, skinned tomatoes
1 onion
1 tablespoon honey
a little butter
pepper

Score the fat of the gammon into diamond shapes. Scatter the sugar and spread the honey over the fat and press in. Grill until the sugared part is golden brown. Place in a buttered casserole, meat side up. On top, place the chopped onions and half the chopped tomatoes, then repeat and season, adding a little white wine. Place a piece of buttered paper on top and cover the casserole with a lid. Cook in a moderate oven for 2 hours. Before serving, strain the juices and thicken with a little flour. Serve with new potatoes and green vegetables. To serve cold, cut into slices with alternate pineapple slices or peach halves. The juices could then be used as stock for soup.

The Pennine Bee Farm, Storey Lane, Ellel, Lancaster, supply English and unusual honeys.

Beef and Ham Roll

1 lb (450 g) lean shoulder steak
½ lb (225 g) ham
1 beaten egg
1 cup breadcrumbs
seasoning
1 teaspoon chopped parsley

Mince the ham and steak and mix with the breadcrumbs, seasoning and chopped parsley. Bind with the beaten egg. Steam in a greased pudding basin for 3½ hours. This goes well with buttered swedes or carrots chopped and well-mashed, boiled onions or spinach.

Venison with Sauce

1 joint of venison
½ pint (300 ml) red wine
1 tablespoon flour
2 teaspoons mashed anchovy
1 teaspoon thyme
1 onion

Rub the joint well with lard as this is a rather dry meat. Cover with foil and roast at 180 C (350 F), allowing 35 minutes to the pound (450 g). Remove the foil towards the end of cooking and allow to brown. Collect the juices from the roast venison and add the chopped onion. Stir In the flour, wine, anchovy and thyme. Cook the sauce until it thickens, stirring continuously, and serve with the venison.

Venison from Rossendale and Bowland Forests was once jealously guarded by Bowbearers and Stewards working for the Lords of the Manor. No large dogs which could threaten the game were allowed. The few remaining herds are today in danger from poachers.

Venison was served in mediaeval halls and castles when those "below the salt" (peasants and serfs) ate "umbles" i.e. the entrails of the deer – thus the expression "eating humble pie".

18th-century Venison Pasty

The words "Venison Pasty" remind us of Robin Hood and his Merry Men, but it must have been convenient "snap" for workmen or walkers out for the day.

about 2 lbs (1 kg) shoulder or breast of venison, cut up
bunch of fresh herbs
ground sea salt and pepper
8 oz (225 g) flaky pastry
2 oz (50 g) butter
2 oz (50 g) seasoned flour
juice of 1 lemon
1 pint (600 ml) stock
a little red wine
1 beaten egg

Cover the meat with seasoned flour. Melt the butter in a pan and brown the meat to seal it. Add the lemon juice, herbs, seasoning and enough stock and red wine to cover the meat. Bring to the boil then simmer gently for 1 ½ hours. Place In a large pie dish and cover with a thick pastry lid brushed with beaten egg. Cook on at 180 C (350 F) until the pastry is browned (about 30 minutes).

Flaky Pastry for Pies & Pasties

8 oz (225 g) flour
6 oz (175 g) lard
1 level teaspoon salt

Use light, quick movements and keep everything cold. Sieve the flour and salt.

Rub a quarter of the lard into the flour and spread it in knobs over the pastry. Fold the pastry into three layers. Seal the edges and roll. Repeat this process until all the lard is worked into the pastry.

To make individual pasties

Roll out the flaky pastry and cut rounds the size of a tea plate. Place portions of cooked venison with juices down the centre. Fold over the other half of the pastry, crimping the outer edges together with a little water. Brush on the glaze of beaten egg which will turn a golden brown in the oven. Place all the pasties on a baking sheet and cook for 30 minutes at 180 C (350 F).

Jugged Hare

There are many variations on jugged hare – the old recipe for Accrington hare or rabbit stew used fresh herbs and parsnips.

---

1 large jointed hare
2 oz (50 g) butter
grated nutmeg
1 pint (600 ml) cider
2 oz (50 g) wholemeal flour
1 dessertspoon Herbes de Provence
1 onion
6 grinds of the peppercorn mill

Clean and cut the hare into small pieces and season each piece. Sprinkle with a little grated nutmeg. Brown the meat in butter and place in a large earthenware pot or jug with sliced onion and herbs. Pour In the cider and cover. Put the pot or jug into a water jacket two-thirds up the sides of the jug. Simmer slowly for three hours, topping up the water to keep up the level.

In a pan stir the flour into the melted butter, adding some of the juices from the hare. Stir till the gravy thickens, giving time for the flour to cook, then pour over the hare and serve with carrots and spinach.

> A wide variety of game, including hares, quail and even smoked quails' eggs can be obtained from Fayre Game Ltd., West Side Industrial Estate, Jackson Street, St. Helens.

Rabbit Hot Pot

---

1 rabbit
seasoned flour
3 small onions
1½ lbs (675 g) potatoes
chopped parsley
water
freshly ground salt and pepper

Wash and joint the rabbit and coat it with seasoned flour. Slice the onions. Peel and cut up the potatoes. Place a layer of onions in an earthenware dish and lay the rabbit on them, sprinkled with seasoning and parsley. Cover with a layer of onions and potatoes. Pour In enough water to cover the rabbit. Cover with a lid or greaseproof paper and cook in a moderate oven for 2 hours.

In 1897 when there were "destructive floods" in Lancashire and Yorkshire, John Dickinson's diary reveals a liking for good dinners: "spare rib of pork, rabbit pie, roast pheasant, roast duck and peas", frequently rounded off with "plum pudding".

Casserole of rabbit

1 rabbit
½ cup fresh breadcrumbs
1 tablespoon rubbed sage
1 tablespoon butter
pepper and salt
the thinly sliced onion rings from 1 large onion

The scant instructions from the 19th century (but easily adapted for today) went as follows:

"Wash and joint a rabbit. Half fill the casserole with water and place the joints of rabbit inside. Add a nut of butter and a good sprinkle of pepper, put salt and rings of onion on top. Cook the covered casserole of rabbit for 1½ hours in a moderate oven."

This basic recipe and ingredients were used by farmers who worked for Sir Peter Hesketh Fleetwood in the early 19th century when Rossall Warren was overrun with rabbits before the town of Fleetwood was built. They had part of their rent remitted for shooting the rabbits. Mr. Vantini, Manager of the North Euston Hotel, is listed in the Certificate Book as supplied with a large plank "for keeping out rabbits".

Pigeon (or Steak) Pie with Forcemeat Balls and Flaky Pastry

An old recipe from Kirkham, where either rooks or plump pigeons were put into pies, directs: "plucking, singeing and drawing . . . Wash pigeons well under cold running water then boil the meat for 30 minutes in ½ pint (300 ml) beef stock. When cool, place the pigeon flesh into a pie dish with the remaining juice and sprinkle with herbs. Put on a pie lid."

Rook shooting was popular in the 1840s, but only the breasts of the birds were used in pies.

Pigeons or steak and other main ingredients:

2 young pigeons or 8 oz (225 g) best steak, cut up
4oz (110 g) mushrooms
4 oz (110 g) bacon
½ pint (300 ml) good beef stock
flour, salt, pepper

Peel and chop the mushrooms, joint the pigeons or cube the steak and cut the bacon into small pieces. Sprinkle the meat with flour, salt and pepper.

Forcemeat Balls:

Next, you have to prepare Forcemeat Balls. These are the additional ingredients needed:

2 teaspoons chopped parsley
½ teaspoon mixed herbs
½ teaspoon grated lemon peel
2 heaped tablespoons of breadcrumbs
½ a beaten egg

To make the balls, mix these ingredients together and bind with half a beaten egg. Form into balls. Put the chopped bacon and mushrooms and some of the forcemeat balls into a pie dish and then add the steak or pigeon joints. Sprinkle with chopped mushrooms and bacon. Fill up with the rest of the forcemeat balls and half fill the dish with stock.

Flaky Pastry for the pie

A flaky pastry top was usual on pigeon pie. Here is a particularly suitable recipe:

8 oz (225 g) flour
6 oz (175 g) butter
¼ pint (150 ml) cold water
pinch of salt

Sift the flour and salt into a basin. Rub 1 oz (25 g) butter into the flour until it resembles breadcrumbs. Gradually add the water, stirring all the time for a good

W. Smith and Sons' butcher shop near Liverpool around the turn of the 19th century proudly displays its Christmas show. Mr. Smith's sons are standing left.

mix. Turn the dough onto à floured board and roll it into a long strip, keeping the sides even and the pastry of uniform thickness.

Divide the rest of the butter into three portions and place one third onto the rolled out pastry by dotting all over with small pieces. Fold the dough over into three layers and roll out. Repeat these actions twice more until all the butter has been well distributed throughout the pastry. Now cut a long, narrow strip of pastry and press it onto the wetted edge of the pie dish. Wet this pastry also and attach it to the rest of the pastry made in a round and shaped to form the lid of the pigeon pie. Decorate with crescent shapes made from any left-over pieces of pastry. Glaze with egg and bake in a moderate oven for 1 ½ hours.

Traditionally, this pie was brought to table with two pigeons' feet in the centre hole of the pie lid.

Duck and Green Peas

This recipe was used in days gone by for preparing an old duck. The Victorian and Edwardian paterfamilias had to excel at carving for a large family. "Spoiling" a hen, "winging" a partridge, "thighing" a woodcock and "embracing" a mallard were some of the grand terms used. 19th century "tracklements" to accompany meat and poultry might be orange, redcurrants or wild raspberries, but orange sauce is today's universal favourite with duck. The real fruit jellies i.e. redcurrant, rowan or rose hip with little sweetening were excellent for cutting any fattiness.

---

1 duck of 3-4 lbs (1.5 kg)
2 oz (50 g) butter
1 lb (450 g) freshly shelled peas
sea salt and peppercorns
1 tablespoon chopped fresh mint
1 egg yolk beaten in a tablespoon of thin cream
1 teaspoon chopped fresh herbs
1 oz (25 g) seasoned flour
2 tablespoons sherry
1 pint (609 ml) stock

Clean the duck well and dust all over with seasoned flour and brown it in the heated butter. Pour off the fat and add sherry, stock and herbs. Sprinkle lightly with ground sea salt and ground peppercorns. Simmer for half an hour. Add the peas and cook for another hour at a steady simmer. The beaten egg and cream are stirred in at the end of cooking and allowed to boil; they make a sauce to serve with the duck and peas. Scatter the tablespoon of freshly chopped mint over the duck before carving.

Chicken with Asparagus Sauce

"Asparagus inspires gentle thoughts," said Charles Lamb, the essayist.

---

3 lbs (1.5 kg) chicken
1 bunch asparagus
4 oz (110 g) petit pois
1 clove of garlic
4 tablespoons double cream
mixed vegetables (1 carrot, 1 leek, 1 celery stalk, 1 onion)
freshly ground salt and black pepper
parsley

Bring a pan of water to the boil. Slice the washed and peeled carrot, leek, celery, garlic clove and onion and place them in the pan with the chicken seasoning and parsley sprigs. Cover and simmer for 50 minutes. Remove the chicken from the pan and, after cooling slightly, slide the meat from the bones and dice it.

The Sauce

Melt 2 oz (50 g) unsalted butter and combine with 3 tablespoons plain flour. Cook for one minute. Remove from heat and stir in 1 pint (600 ml) of the vegetable stock. Bring to the boil and simmer for 10 minutes.

After removing the woody stalk ends, wash the asparagus and cut into short pieces. Add the petit pois and simmer for 6 minutes. Drain and add to the sauce. Simmer gently for another minute then stir in the double cream. This smooth, white sauce enriched with cream is poured over the chicken.

> The famous Goosnargh duck and chicken can be purchased from Johnson and Swarbrick's farm, Goosnargh Lane, Goosnargh, near Preston. The birds are reared on foodstuffs free from chemicals and growth powders. Heathcote's famous restaurants serve Johnson and Swarbrick's poultry.

Chicken in Aspic

¼ oz (5 g) gelatine

2 tablespoons water

4 oz (110 g) cooked chicken

2 hard-boiled eggs

$1/_3$ pint (200 ml) chicken stock

2 oz (50 g) cooked peas

Slice the eggs and place then in the bottom of a tin mould. Add the cooked peas then the chicken in small pieces. Put the water and gelatine in a pan and melt over low heat. Make the stock from a chicken stock cube and sieve into the gelatine. Cover the mixture in the mould with this liquid and when cool, chill in the fridge. Serve sliced with a fresh green salad.

A Suitable Tossed Spring Salad

a bunch of watercress

a little cucumber

Spring onions

Wash everything. Chop the onions and cucumber and place in a dish with the watercress.

The Dressing

Toss the salad in a dressing made from:

1½ tablespoons olive oil

½ tablespoon vinegar

a little pepper and salt

a pinch of dry mustard

Turkey Breast Steaks with Juniper Cream

This tasty recipe by Marie Sherratt can be enjoyed separate from the festive season. The juniper cream with its subtle flavour offers a nice change from cranberry sauce.

---

4 turkey breasts – approx. 1 lb (450 g)

2 tablespoons virgin olive oil

1 tablespoon unsalted butter

2 oz (50 g) finely sliced mushrooms

2 oz (50 g) finely chopped onion

¼ pint (150 ml) turkey or chicken stock

3 tablespoons sherry

12 juniper berries lightly crushed

zest of 1 orange

¼ pint (150 ml) double cream

freshly ground black pepper and salt

Heat I tablespoon of olive oil and butter in an ovenproof casserole dish. Put in the turkey steaks and turn them over to seal both sides. Bake in the centre of the oven at 200 C (400 F) for 25 minutes. Add the stock, sherry, crushed juniper berries, orange zest and cook for 8-10 minutes until reduced by half. Add the cream slowly and season to taste. Re-heat, but do not boil. Surround the turkey steaks with the gently cooked mushrooms and onions and serve with new or mashed potatoes and vegetables.

Turkey Gravy

To serve six when Christmas does come round. Grandad Ramsey called this Giblet Gravy and no Christmas was complete without this and a hand-raised pork pie.

4 tablespoons vegetable oil
giblets and trimmings from the turkey
2 large onions, chopped finely
4 carrots peeled and chopped finely
2 bay leaves
2 celery stalks peeled and chopped finely
8 black peppercorns
¼ pint (150 ml) white wine
1 teaspoon dried sage
1 sprig of parsley
1½ oz (40 g) unsalted butter
1½ oz (40 g) plain flour

Chop the trimmings and roast in 2 tablespoons of the oil for half an hour in a moderate even. Heat the rest of the oil in a pan and cook the vegetables until they turn brown. Add the wine, trimmings and giblets, bay leaves, sage and parsley. Cover with hot water and bring to the boil. Reduce the heat to a low simmer for 3 hours. Strain and skim off any fat, then boil rapidly until you have about I pint (600 ml) of stock. Melt the butter in another pan and stir in the flour. Cook gently then add the stock, stirring well. Simmer for 20 minutes then finally grind in the peppercorns.

Stewed Tripe and Onions

1 lb (450 g) honeycomb tripe
½ pint (300 ml) milk
2 Spanish onions
pepper, salt, vinegar
1 oz (25 g) butter
pinch of nutmeg
1 oz (25 g) flour
slice of toast

Cut the tripe into small pieces. Skin the onions, scald them and cut them into quarters. Put them into a saucepan, cover with water and simmer slowly for two hours. Add the tripe and simmer for a further 15 minutes. Mix the flour to a smooth cream with the milk and add to the saucepan. Stir until the flour thickens. Add seasoning and butter cut into small pieces. Cook all together for a few minutes. Serve very hot, garnished with sippets of toast.

A whiter, even more nourishing version, was achieved by stewing entirely in milk. This was known rather vulgarly in Burnley and Blackburn as "a bottle of titty". A de luxe version used ¼ pint (150 ml) of cream and was dished up with the rind of half a lemon and sprigs of parsley.

Tripe and Cow Heel Stew

3 lbs (1.5 kg) tripe
sprig of thyme
1 cow heel
2 large carrots
3 cloves
3 onions
1 cupful of water
seasoning

Cut the tripe and cow heel into small pieces. Prepare the carrots and onions and cut them into thin slices. Into a stew jar place a layer of prepared vegetables and put some of the cow heel and tripe on top. Repeat these layers, finishing off with vegetables. Add the thyme and cloves and sprinkle with salt and pepper. Pour on the cupful of water and cover securely. Stand the jar in a saucepan of water and keep this slowly boiling for 1½ hours, from time to time adding more water as it boils down. Allow the jar to stand for a short time before serving the stew.

"We have ways of making your tripe ..." — 99, it would seem, from a Report issued in 1932 by United Cattle Products Ltd., Manchester. This famous food was prized in Lancashire for cheapness and high nourishment value. It has a remarkable history dating from the Romans who set great store by it. U.C.P.'s advice was: "Be generous with pepper, salt and vinegar and if served hot, let it be really hot." One famous cook, Miss Florence B. Jack, compared it favourably with the rich man's oyster at the time of this report.

Ox Cheek

---

2 lbs (900 g) ox cheek
1 pint (600 ml) stock
1 teaspoon malt vinegar
8 oz (225 g) onions
2 leeks
2 carrots
2 turnips
8 oz (225 g) potatoes
1 oz (25 g) beef dripping
seasoning

Well wash the portions of ox cheek and cut into slices. Melt the dripping in a stew pan and put in the slices of ox. Fry until slightly brown. Add the sliced carrots, stock and vinegar. Season and simmer. After an hour's simmering put in the well-washed, cut up leeks and turnips. Peel the potatoes and add these whole. Continue cooking for another hour until all the vegetables are done. If desired, dumplings can also be cooked along with the rest in the last half hour.

If you have difficulty in finding ox cheek these days, use some good stewing steak instead.

Granny Brown's Braised Ox Tongue – a recipe dating back to the 1840s

Wash and dry one salted ox tongue after soaking overnight in water. Prepare a "mirepoix" of vegetables consisting of 2 carrots, 2 small turnips, 2 onions, a stalk of celery, 2 cloves, bouquet garni, ground sea salt and 1 oz (25 g) of butter.

Heat the butter and add the vegetables peeled, washed and cut into pieces. Fry gently. Add the bouquet garni and place all in an earthenware dish. Put in the tongue and pour over all 2 pints (1200 ml) of brown stock which has been brought to the boil. Put the lid on the earthenware dish and place in a hot oven. After 10 minutes reduce the heat and cook slowly for 5 hours until the tongue is tender.

Remove from the dish. Cut away gristle at the root of the tongue and pull out any bones. If the tongue is sufficiently cooked all the skin slides off easily. Place the tongue in curled shape in a round tin or casserole. Cover with 1 pint (600 ml) of stock to which has been added ¼ oz (5 g) of gelatine. Cover with greaseproof paper and press down with a heavy weight. After allowing the dish to stand thus for 24 hours, the tongue can be turned out, sliced and served with salad.

Ox Roasting Team, Rawtenstall, with Mr. Eastwood far right. An old diary entry of 1887 states: "On Jubilee Day for Victoria, beacons were fired and a fire of ling kindled on the fell looked weird. There was fiddle and dancing."

Desserts

This photograph of the cook and two maids, a great array of pans and utensils on the shelves behind them, indicates the kitchen of a large house early in the 20th century. Far right is the Bain Marie, a shallow, wide tin containing warm water which held lidded pots in various sizes.

Snow Pancakes

This very old recipe is from the days when snow could be relied upon to fall on Pancake Tuesday (Shrove Tuesday). In the country, freshly fallen snow was then clean enough to collect. My grandmother used 3 tablespoons of snow in her pancakes, along with:

---

3 tablespoons flour
1 large egg
butter for greasing
½ pint (300 ml) milk

Gradually mix the flour with the milk and the well-beaten egg. Just before frying, add the snow. Beat all together.

Brush a small frying pan with melted butter and "flow in" a dessertspoon of the batter. Tilt the pan to spread it evenly and brown quickly and lightly on high heat. Toss, to do the other side.

Fill a heated dish with the pancakes, dust caster sugar between each layer and eat with lemon juice well-sprinkled over each pancake.

On Shrove Tuesday in the ancient market town of Poulton-le-Fylde the Pancake Bell was rung to call apprentices from work "and prepared to eat their pancakes". They went through the town from house to house begging the sweetmeat. Some think the story goes back further to an occasion when furious Poulton women routed a group of invading Danes with their frying pans.

Old-Fashioned Syllabub

Real Old English Syllabub was made with milk straight from the cow into the wine or brandy to produce a frothy mixture that was sweetened and spiced. "Fresh from the cow" milk is not widely available today, but its frothiness caused by flowing straight from the udder helped in producing a light and airy syllabub.

For a modern-day version, soak the grated rind of one lemon in its own juice for 2 hours, then add:

---

3 oz (75 g) caster sugar
2 tablespoons brandy
2 tablespoons sherry
½ pint (300 ml) of whipped double cream

Gently blend the sugar, brandy and sherry into the whipped cream. Put the mixture into goblets and chill.

Redcurrant Syllabub

---

2 egg whites
2 dessertspoons redcurrant jelly
1 pint (600 ml) cream
2 oz (50 g) caster sugar
¼ pint (150 ml) white wine
grated rind of 1 orange

Beat the cream with the wine and sugar. Stir in the rind. Spoon the mixture into a large bowl. Beat the egg.whites and the redcurrant jelly together until stiff and spoon this on top of the wine and cream. Serve with ratafia biscuits or macaroons.

Orange and Ginger Sweet

If required for four people allow 6 juicy oranges and a tablespoon of chopped stem ginger. A dessertspoon of soft brown sugar is optional. Peel and thinly slice the oranges into a glass dish and scatter the ginger between layers. Sprinkle with the sugar and a small quantity of syrup juice from the stem ginger jar. Leave for at least an hour to marinate before serving. During the war years, when oranges were almost unobtainable, this was a rare treat.

Victoria Plum Slices

These delicious plums appeared as Harvest Festivals loomed. At one such Service, the organist at Chadderton Church suddenly noticed a field mouse creeping from a sheaf of corn. Fortunately, the ladies' choir was blissfully unaware and sang "All is safely gathered in."

---

6 Victoria plums
4 oz (110 g) softened butter
1 free range egg
4 oz (110 g) caster sugar
8 oz (225 g) self raising flour
½ teaspoon vanilla essence
1 tablespoon plum jam
1 oz (25 g) flaked almonds

Grease a 10 ins (25.5 cm) x 7 ins (18 cm) cake tin. Beat the butter and sugar until pale. Add the egg and vanilla essence. Stir in the sifted flour and pour the mixture into the tin. Wash, dry and slice the plums and place them cut side up in the sponge mixture. Sprinkle with flaked almonds and bake for 30 minutes in a moderate oven. Whilst still warm, brush with the plum jam to glaze.

Pears in Ginger Syrup

¼ pint (150 ml) white wine
¼ pint (150 ml) water
4 oz (110 g) sugar
4 tablespoons ginger wine
1 cinnamon stick
3 tablespoons almonds
4 pears
fresh cream

Put all the liquids into an enamel pan with the sugar and cinnamon. Heat very gently until the sugar has dissolved. Peel the pears and cut the bases so that they stand upright, but do not remove the stalks. Place the pears in the liquid and simmer gently for 20 minutes. Transfer the pears to a serving dish, then boil the liquid until it becomes syrupy. Remove the cinnamon stick and pour the syrup over the pears. Allow to cool, then chill for 8 hours, occasionally spooning the syrup over the pears. Scatter on almonds and serve with cream.

Chocolate Mousse

This recipe comes from one of Lancashire's Country Houses, Meols Hall, near Southport, courtesy of Lady Mary Hesketh.

2 slabs of dark chocolate
2 tablespoons of orange juice
4 eggs
2 oz (50 g) roasted chopped nuts

Melt the chocolate with the orange juice in a Bain Marie (or, in a dish over a pan of boiling water) stirring until it is like very thick cream. Allow it to cool. Separate the eggs and stir the yolks into the chocolate. Whip the whites very stiff and fold into the chocolate. Pour into a soufflé dish and leave overnight in the fridge. When set, scatter the nuts over the mousse.

Chocolate Pots

Both this and the previous sweets are indulgent treats for tired "singles" to wind up a hard day's work. They can be kept in the fridge for use on subsequent days.

3 oz (75 g) plain chocolate
3 medium free range eggs
¼ pint (150 ml) fresh double cream
1 oz (25 g) butter
1 tablespoon warm water

Break up the chocolate and put into a basin standing over a pan of hot water. Add the butter and leave until both ingredients have melted, stirring twice. Beat in the strained egg yolks. When smooth, remove from heat and stir in the warm water. Beat the egg whites until stiff, then fold into the chocolate mixture. Transfer to 4 sundae dishes and chill. When ready to serve, whip the cream and use to decorate.

Pies and Puddings

"Who said peacock pie?" asked poet Walter de la Mare. This peacock, Percy of Singleton, is well-protected. No longer can peacocks and swans be roasted, put into pies and brought to groaning refectory tables, decorated with their claws and magnificent tail feathers. Much photographed, Percy consistently refuses "to display". And can you blame him? Ancestors are doubtless whispering "Beware" as he stalks through the beautiful garden or perches in the trees, plumage safe.

Christmas Pie

"Mince pie, the favourite treat of Christmas, made of a compound of eastern productions, represented the offerings of the wise men who came bringing spices. Its old English coffin shape was in imitation of the manger in which the infant Jesus was laid." (1837)

This de luxe version is well worth the extra time spent.

Make a short crust pastry with 6 oz (175 g) flour, 3 oz (75 g) butter, a pinch of salt and cold water to mix.

Cover a greased pie plate with pastry and cover the pastry generously with mincemeat.

Cream together 2½ oz (65 g) sugar and 2 oz (50 g) butter. Add I well-beaten egg. Mix 2 oz (50 g) of soft cake crumbs with 2 on (50 g) ground almonds. Add this to the butter, sugar and egg mixture and spread it over the mincemeat. Bake in a moderate oven for 30 minutes.

Steamed Marmalade Pudding

3 oz (75 g) butter

1 orange

3 oz (75 g) caster sugar

2 beaten free range eggs

3 oz (75 g) wholemeal flour

2 tablespoons orange marmalade

3 tablespoons milk

Grease a I ½ pint (900 ml) pudding basin. Peel and thinly slice the orange. Line the basin with these slices, pressing them gently on the grease. Cream the butter and sugar until fluffy, add the eggs and fold in the flour, marmalade and milk. Beat all well together. Gradually pour this mixture into the basin., and cover with greaseproof paper. Place on an upturned saucer in a large pan of boiling water and steam for 2 hours, topping up the water as it evaporates.

The pudding can be served with a plain cornflour sauce or an orange sauce made by adding the juice of one orange and its grated rind to the plain sauce.

Cornflour Sauce

1 oz (25 g) patent cornflour

1 oz (25 g) sugar

¾ pint (450 ml) milk

Blend the cornflour and sugar with 2 tablespoons of milk. Heat the rest of the milk in a pan until it bolls. Pour in the cornflour and continue to stir until the sauce thickens. Stir on for a further two minutes to ensure that the cornflour is cooked.

Ginger Pudding

3 oz (75 g) margarine
4 tablespoons self raising flour
2 tablespoons golden syrup
1 egg
2 teaspoons ground ginger
1 oz (25 g) brown sugar
a little milk

Cream the margarine and sugar together Beat the egg and add to the mixture, Stir in the flour and ginger. Add the syrup and milk last and mix all the ingredients very well together.

Grease a pudding basin and put in the mixture. Cover with foil or greaseproof paper and steam for 1½ hours.

Fleetwood Pudding for two

2 slices of bread, grated
2 egg yolks
½ pint (300 ml) milk
2 oz (50 g) sugar

Beat the egg yolks with the milk and sugar. Put the grated bread in an oven-proof dish and pour on the beaten egg mixture. Use the egg whites to make meringue topping. Cook in a moderate oven until the meringue is browned.

In the 1900s, what became an interesting landmark at Clifton near the River Irwell, was nicknamed "T' Puddin' lamp" when Robin Pit improved production. Two large stones cut to resemble two halves of pudding were fitted round the base of the main Pit Head Lamp to protect it from carts at the loading stage.

Noddy Pudding

This 19th-century name comes from the April 1st tradition because the Holy Bible states: "He that calleth his brother a fool is in danger of hell fire." Some of our ancestors observed this and substituted Noddy for fool, my Sunday School teacher being one.

Opinions vary on this recipe which seems to be more of a cake than a pudding, but most agree that the whiteness of this cake-cum-puddding symbolised Easter purity and, although Easter is a moveable feast, April is not far away.

4 oz (110 g) butter
7 oz (200 g) caster sugar
8 oz (225 g) plain flour
a few drops of vanilla essence
3 beaten egg whites
2½ teaspoons baking powder
¼ pint (150 ml) skimmmed milk

Cream the butter and sugar together and beat in the vanilla essence. Sift the plain flour with the baking powder. Add the flour gradually with the skimmed milk then fold in the 3 stiffly beaten egg whites. Put the mixture in an 8 inch (20 cm) lined cake tin and bake in a moderate oven for 40 minutes. When cold, cover with white icing.

Rhubarb Crumble

1½ lbs (675 g) rhubarb
6 oz (175 g) brown sugar
6 oz (175 g) plain flour
3 oz (75 g) butter
2 oz (50 g) caster sugar

Cut the rhubarb into small lengths and place in a pie dish with a little water and 4 oz (110 g) of the brown sugar. Rub the butter into the flour and mix in the caster sugar. Spread this crumble mixture over the rhubarb. Sprinkle the remaining brown sugar on top. Bake in a moderate oven for 50 minutes.

Apple Charlotte

4 oz (110 g) breadcrumbs
1 lb (450 g) Bramley apples, peeled, cored and sliced
4 oz (110 g) brown sugar
grated rind of 1 large lemon
2 oz (50 g) butter
2 tablespoons water

Grease a pie dish thickly with butter. Cover with a good layer of brown sugar.

Stirring the Christmas Pudding in Victorian times. Each child was allowed to stir vigorously and make a silent wish. The same performance took place when the mincemeat was being prepared some weeks before the festive season began.

Add alternate layers of apples and breadcrumbs until the dish is full, the last layer being breadcrumbs. Add the rest of the sugar, grated rind and cut-up butter, leaving a little butter to dot the top. Pour on the water. Bake for 1 hour in a moderate oven.

Christmas Pudding

---

4 oz (110 g) sultanas

4 oz (110 g) currants

4 oz (110 g) raisins

2 oz (50 g) candied peel

2 oz (50 g) chopped almonds

4 oz (110 g) plain flour

4 oz (110 g) brown breadcrumbs

1 carrot freshly grated

¼ teaspoon cinnamon

3 fl oz (75 ml) sherry

½ teaspoon mixed spice

3 free range eggs

4 oz (110 g) demerara sugar

3 tablespoons brandy

grated rind and juice of 1 lemon

1 apple cored and grated

4 oz (110 g) grated suet

Put all the ingredients in a large bowl and mix well, first the dry ingredients then the sherry, brandy and well-beaten eggs. (My grandmother soaked the raisins, currants and sultanas in brandy for a few days before the pudding was made, as she did with the Christmas Cake fruit.)

Well grease a large pudding basin and put in the mixture. Cover with 4 thicknesses of greaseproof paper and tie up the basin in a pudding cloth ready for steaming. The Christmas Pudding requires steaming for 8 hours, 6 to cook it and 2 hours extra on Christmas Day itself.

De Luxe Christmas Pudding

---

1 packet dried fruit salad
2 handfuls washed raisins and sultanas
10 stoned "box" dates
6 slices of bread
freshly grated nutmeg
finely grated rind of a fresh lemon
juice of 1 large orange
1 tablespoon chopped stem ginger

Soak the dried fruit overnight but keep the stem ginger in its syrup. Next day cut the fruit into small pieces. Cook in a pan of water for 20 minutes with the spice and lemon rind. Add the orange juice. If desired, sweeten with I dessertspoon brown sugar.

Cut the crusts off the bread and line the pudding basin well with this bread. Add the ginger. Spoon in the fruit and make a bread "lid". Cover with a plate slightly smaller than the circumference of the basin so that the pudding can be weighted down. Weight it down for 8 hours until the bread is completely soaked with the fruit juices.

Serve with natural yoghurt or cream. More stem ginger in its syrup is another optional extra. After all, it is Christmas!

Sticky Toffee Pudding

---

2 oz.(50 g) butter
6 oz (175 g) granulated sugar
8 oz (225 g) flour
1 teaspoon baking powder
6 oz (175 g) stoned dates
1 egg
1 teaspoon vanilla essence
1 teaspoon bicarbonate of soda
½ pint (300 ml) boiling water

Cream the butter and sugar together. Sift the flour and baking powder. Beat the whisked egg into the creamed mixture with some of the flour. Continue beating for 2 minutes before adding the rest of the flour.

A wedding in Longridge c.1900 followed by a lavish reception and feast, although quite modest compared with the unprecedented celebrations when Lady Elizabeth Egerton, daughter of the Earl of Wilton, married Captain Dudley Charles Fitzgerald de Ros in 1853. Triumphal arches marked the route to Prestwich Church which was lined by 1,000 children. A beribboned ox with gilded horns was roasted, a 21-gun salute was fired and the church bells rang all day. Local butcher John Clough, who presided over the ox roasting, handed out slices to the poor, who drank several casks of ale. The day ended with a Ball at Heaton Hall.

Lightly flour the dates and chop them well. Pour the boiling water over them.

Mix in the bicarbonate of soda and vanilla essence. Add this to the mixture and blend all well. Turn into a buttered cake tin and bake for 40 minutes in a moderate oven.

The Toffee Coating

2½ oz (65 g) brown sugar

1½ oz (40 g) butter

2 tablespoons double cream

Beat the brown sugar, butter and cream and simmer for 3 minutes. Pour it over the hot pudding and place under the grill until the toffee coating gently bubbles. As this burns easily, it needs careful timing.

Sultana and Almond Slice

---

4 oz (110 g) sultanas

2 oz (50 g) ground almonds

¾ oz (20 g) caster sugar

¾ oz (20 g) icing sugar

1 beaten free range egg

7½ oz (215 g) pack of frozen puff pastry, defrosted

Mix the sultanas, almonds and sugars. Add the egg to bind the mixture. Roll out the pastry to 14 ins (36 cm) x 8 ins (20 cm) and cut in half. Place one half on a baking sheet and spread the filling to about ½ inch (1 cm) of the edge. Dampen the edge. Place the other half of the pastry on top and press the edges together. Slit the top of the pastry and brush with beaten egg. Bake in a pre-heated oven at 220 C (425 F) for 20 minutes until risen. Serve with yoghurt.

Hazelnut Pie

---

8 oz (225 g) wholemeal flour 4 oz (100g) margarine

8 oz (225 g) hazelnuts

2 oz (50 g) unsalted butter

2 oz (50 g) Barbados sugar

3 medium eggs, beaten

6 oz (175 g) acacia honey

juice of half a lemon

2 egg whites stiffly beaten

Pre-heat the oven to 230 C (450 F).

Line a greased tin with the pastry made from the flour and margarine. Chop the hazelnuts finely. Beat the butter and sugar and gradually add the beaten egg.

Add the honey and lemon juice and keep beating until the mixture is frothy. Fold in the hazelnuts then the egg whites. Pour the mixture into the pastry case. Bake for 10 minutes then reduce the heat to 180 C (350 F) for a further 25 minutes. Serve the pie quite cold with thin cream.

Morris dancers at the Carleton Gala, June 1929. Harry Gleave is on the right of the front row. They trained long and hard for the procession and were rewarded with home-made lemonade. Summer Pudding was a favourite in the village as so many had fruit gardens behind the cottages.

Summer Pudding

The delicious summer puddings of old used 2 lbs (900 g) of fresh fruit.

---

4 oz (110 g) redcurrants

4 oz (110 g) blackcurrants

(In each case separate the berries from the stalks with a fork.)

4 oz (110 g) golden yellow gooseberries ("honeyberries"),
topped and tailed

8 oz (225 g) raspberries (hulled)

8 oz (225 g) strawberries (hulled)

4 oz (110 g) dessert apples peeled, cored and thinly sliced

6 oz (175 g) caster sugar

8 thin slices of bread, crusts removed

Grease the sides of a 1 ½ pint (900 ml) pudding bowl with butter. Make a base with one slice of bread, then overlap the other slices round the sides. Leave no gaps. Gently pour in the lightly cooked fruit. Make a lid with the remaining bread slices. Rest a saucer on top and weigh it down with an 8 oz (225 g) weight. Put in the f ridge when cold and leave for two days.. Serve portions with whipped double cream or yoghurt.

Jam Roly-Poly

8 oz (225 g) flour

4 oz (110 g) shredded suet

1 teaspoon baking powder

cold water to mix jam

Sieve the flour and the baking powder together. Add the finely chopped suet. Mix to a stiff dough with a little cold water. Roll out the suet crust pastry into an oblong shape. Spread it generously with jam to within I inch (2.5 cm) of the edges. Moisten these edges with cold water and roll up tightly. Wrap in a greaseproof paper and pudding cloth and steam for 2½ hours. Serve with custard or yoghurt. Any good-flavoured jam will serve but home-made is best,

Manchester Baked Custard

1 pint (600 ml) milk

4 tablespoons sugar

4 egg yolks

1 vanilla pod to flavour the milk

nutmeg

Beat the yolks and sugar together and boil the milk containing the vanilla pod. Remove the pod carefully and save it in a polythene bag. Pour the boiling milk over the yolk mixture, stirring constantly. Strain, then turn into a large buttered dish.

Bake in a moderate oven for 25 minutes. Sprinkle with grated nutmeg.

A Manchester lady reports that true "Manchester Tart" should be baked in a pastry case with jam spread at the bottom. I would recommend brushing the pastry first with egg white and allowing this to dry before adding the custard. This will prevent a soggy base. Personally, I think the jam is better in a "butty"!

Bread

"After dinner I worked bread then came and mended stockings beside William. He fell asleep." (Dorothy Wordsworth's Journal) 1771-1855.

Paddling on Blackpool beach c 1900. J. Singleton's bathing machines advertise: "Eat Hovis bread, the best of all breads." Early visitors to Blackpool came on foot or in carts. The "Pad jammers" from Padiham brought their own food in hampers, with water bottles slung underneath their carts. Later they came in trainloads and the first trips arranged by philanthropic mill owners for their workers might feature literally a wagon load of food. One such mill owner filled a wagon with simple bread and cheese to feed the multitude on arrival.

These occasions were well-organised. Marquees were set up for the issue of food and drink. The Preston and Wyre Railway Company issued pamphlets with instructions to the workers to arrive in good time and bring no intoxicants. They gave information on interesting things to look out for on the journey and where temperance drinks were obtainable. It was discovered on the Females' Trip that some men had dressed as women and infiltrated in order to get a free ride. As for the water bottles slung under the carts, some went back to Padiham full of sea water because "physick from the sea" was judged by leading doctors in the late 18th and early 19th centuries' to be highly beneficial and during their stay Lancashire lads and lasses drank it daily.

Wholemeal Bread

1½ lbs (675 g) brown wholemeal flour
1 oz (25 g) lard
½ oz (15 g) yeast
½ pint (450 ml) water
1 teaspoon salt

Mix the flour and salt and rub in the lard. Blend the fresh yeast with a little warm water and add to the flour mixture. Mix to a pliable dough. Turn onto a lightly floured surface and knead for 10 minutes.

Place the dough in a greased bowl and put the bowl into a large oiled polythene bag. Leave this in a warm place until the dough has doubled in size. Turn the dough onto a lightly floured surface and knead for a further six minutes. Grease three 1 lb (450 g) tins and divide the dough into three equal pieces. Place in the loaf tins and put each into oiled polythene bags until the tops of the loaves become rounded. This needs about 30 minutes in a warm place.

Remove the bags and bake in a pre-heated oven at 230 C (450 F) for 30 minutes. When the base of the loaf is tapped it should sound hollow.

Wholemeal Harvest Loaves

3 lbs (1.5 kg) Stoneground wholemeal flour
1 oz (25 g) dried yeast
1 crushed vitamin C tablet
1 oz (25 g) lard
1 tablespoon brown sugar
1 dessertspoon salt
1¾ pints (1 litre) warm water

Pre-heat the oven to 230 C (450 F).

Crush the vitamin C tablet into the sugar and place in a bowl with a third of the warm water. Into this whisk the dried yeast. Cover and leave in a warm place. In a large mixing bowl place the flour, salt and lard. Rub the lard into the flour, stir in the yeast mixture and mix all thoroughly with the flat of the hand. Stand the bowl in the remaining warm water. After 5 minutes turn the dough onto a floured surface and knead it well for 10 minutes, then divide the dough into two large and two small pieces. Place a small piece on a large piece to form the traditional cottage loaf shape. With the handle of a wooden spoon, make a

Staining Windmill in the Fylde or "cornfield" of Lancashire. Wheat for frumenty was collected here and flour was milled for bread-making.

hole centrally which penetrates the large piece of dough to a depth of 1 inch (2.5 cm). Cover with a damp tea towel and leave to rise for 30 minutes. Bake at 230 C (450 F) for 35 minutes.

Oat Bran Muffins

9 oz (250 g) oat bran
1 tablespoon baking powder
2 oz (50 g) sultanas
½ pint (300 ml) milk
2 oz (50 g) brown sugar
2 egg whites
2 tablespoons olive oil
1 teaspoon cinnamon

Mix together the oat bran, sugar, baking powder, cinnamon and sultanas. Mix the milk, oil and egg white and pour onto the mixed dry ingredients. Leave to stand for 5 minutes then put the mixture into paper bun cases on a baking sheet and cook for 15 minutes in a moderate oven. This high-fibre cereal (Mornflake Oatbran is of International Gold Medal Quality) may help to reduce cholesterol as part of a low-fat diet.

In the 1800s, enough bread and "oven-bottom" muffins had to be baked at home to last the family a week. In Bolton in 1876 however, Ellen Warburton had a bright idea. Rising early, she made four loaves and six cakes, using 6 lbs of flour in the oven at her Bolton corner shop. She sold all within an hour of opening. Business expanded. Her nephew, Henry Warburton, became the baker and for six nights a week he slept on a makeshift bed at Ellen's shop. "He never took his work clothes off from Monday till Saturday." And that is how Warburton's Bread of Bolton was born. At their centenary, they celebrated a turnover of £25 million.

Tea Bread

---

1 lb (450 g) self raising flour

1 teaspoon salt

2 oz (50 g) lard

1 oz (25 g) sugar

3 oz (75 g) currants

1 oz (25 g) chopped peel

½ pint (300 ml) milk

Mix the flour and salt in a basin and rub in the lard. Stir in the sugar, currants and peel. Mix into a dough with the milk. Turn onto a floured board and form a round. Place in a well-greased, round cake tin and brush over with milk. Bake in a moderate oven for 1 hour. Instead of currants and peel, figs or dates may be used to make Fig or Date Bread.

Around the turn of the 19th century, tea gardens became popular. Young ladies in long, white aprons and straw "boater hats" served strawberries and cream within the garden. Drinks were advertised on the exterior walls of wooden temperance huts: "Rowntree's Cocoa; Dainty Cups of Mazawattee Tea; Iced Oxo and Soda, cooling and delicious". You could have as many strawberries as you could eat, for behind the Gardens were extensive strawberry fields. At Fleetwood, these stretched from the Strawberry Gardens Hotel on Poulton Road to the sea shore.

Real Hot Cross Buns

Although supermarkets sell hot cross buns from Christmas onwards, traditionally they were eaten (spiced, hot and buttered) only on Good Friday, the tops marked with a cross to commemorate Christ's death on the cross. Three hundred years ago spiced breads could be sold only at Christmas and Good Friday.

My great-grandfather was a master baker at Waterfoot and was up at 4 a.m. to make "real hot cross buns" for Good Friday's treat.

---

6 oz (175 g) wholemeal flour

11 oz (300 g) strong white flour

3 teaspoons mixed spice

2 oz (50 g) muscovado sugar

1 oz (25 g) fresh yeast

2 oz (50 g) melted butter

½ pint (300 ml) warm water

1 large free range egg

1 tablespoon honey

3 oz (75 g) each of washed sultanas and finely cut candied
peel – 6 oz (175 g) in total

Mix the flours, sugar and spice in a large bowl. In a small dish mix the yeast with the honey. Pour in the warm water and one tablespoon of the mixed flour. After mixing well leave in a warm place.

After about 10 minutes, when the yeast starts bubbling, add it to the flour plus the egg and melted butter. Beat all with a wooden spoon. Mix in the fruit then cover the bowl in a warm place.

In 2 hours the dough will have doubled in size to be light and soft. On a floured board cut it into 15 pieces, gently form into bun shape and place on greased baking sheets. Cover with a damp cloth and again put to "prove" (rise) in a warm place for 15 minutes. Brush each bun with beaten egg and place 2 strips of pastry on top to form a cross. Bake in a hot oven for 25 minutes.

An Edwardian bridal cake. Cooks stood on high stools to spin sugar into fanciful concoctions. In 1840 at a banquet at the North Euston Hotel, Mrs. Sharples bore in "a cake of the new port of Fleetwood at large".

Cakes & Biscuits

Parson and poet Robert Herrick (1591-1674) wrote:

"I sing of May Poles, Hock-Carts, Wassails and Wakes,
Of Bridegrooms, Brides and of their Bridal cakes."

Wakes involved fasting, an honouring of the local saint, followed by feasting, a time when villagers remembered the dead and even forecast those who would die in the year to come – hence soul-caking. Wassails spelled Christmas. May Poles meant times of great rejoicing because the earth had woken up again to give forth fruits after barren winter. In the following Lancashire recipes, cakes symbolise events going back hundreds of years.

Eccles Cakes

¼ lb (110 g) flaky pastry
½ oz (15 g) melted margarine
½ oz (15 g) candied peel
1 oz (25 g) granulated sugar
2 oz (50 g) currants
pinch of nutmeg

Mix together the melted margarine, currants, nutmeg, chopped peel and sugar. Roll out the pastry thinly and cut into rounds about 6 ins (I 5 cm) in diameter. Place a portion of the mixture on each round. Dampen the edges of the pastry and gather them together. Pat into rounds and snip each top gently with scissors. Brush with milk and sprinkle with sugar. Bake in a hot oven for 20 minutes.

Since 1893 "real original Eccles Cakes" were baked at Mr. Wardle's shop, "Ye Olde Thatche". They were made from flaky pastry and currants. Mr. Wardle also sold home-made ice cream from these centuries-old premises.

Goosnargh Cakes

---

7 oz (200 g) plain flour

5 oz (150 g) fresh butter

2 oz (50 g) grated loaf sugar

1 teaspoon coriander seeds

caster sugar for dusting one eighth of an inch thick

Rub the butter into the flour then stir in the sugar and coriander seeds. Leave in a cool place for four hours. Knead the mixture lightly together. Roll out and form into small, round cakes. Bake in a cool oven for one hour. Dust thickly with caster sugar when cool.

The famous Goosnargh Cakes were sold in the late 19th century by Mr. and Mrs. Clegg of Sandbank Farm, Goosnargh, and were still being made by Mrs. Clegg, a descendant, in the 1930s. Mentioned in the Domesday Book, Goosnargh (Anglo-Saxon for Gorse Green), was for centuries known only for its annual feast, when crowds arrived for the cake eating. One Whitsuntide 50,000 cakes were sold. Every inn employed a woman to bake them. At the Bushells Arms Mrs. Bramwell scraped away on a yard-long grater for the sugar (called loaf sugar) used in the recipe.

Ye Horns Inn, Goosnargh, with a history dating back to 1782 and at one time known as The Roebuck Inn (there were antlers above the entrances), still has original oak beams and open fires. Traditional food served by Chef/Proprietor Mark Woods includes roast duckling, pheasant in season and, of course, Goosnargh Cakes.

Tosset Cakes

1 lb (450 g) plain flour
1 lb (450 g) butter
¼ lb (110 g) raw cane sugar
1 teaspoon caraway seeds
1 teaspoon coriander seeds
icing sugar in a dredger
caster sugar in a dredger

Crush the seeds with a rolling pin or pestle. Rub the butter into the flour, add the sugar and the crushed seeds and leave in a cool larder ovemight, then knead and roll out to a quarter inch thickness. Make small cakes, using a pastry cutter on a floured baking board and sprinkle each tosset cake generously with caster sugar. Bake in a cool oven for one hour until firm. The cakes should not brown. Dredge thickly with icing sugar and store in an air-tight tin.

These spicy, sugary cakes were traditionally eaten in Stalmine, Over-Wyre, the weekend after August 12th on Tosset Sunday. The old name of the church was St. Oswald and "Tosset" makes affectionate reference to the saint.

Father's Sadcake

No recipe survives, but word of mouth and proof of mother's cooking make if easy to remember. The basis was a good shortcrust pastry made with lard, but perfection requires baking in an old-fashioned fire oven, which we are unlikely to see again. The pastry was rolled out and heaped with currants, raisins and sugar, with a little water sprinkled on. The edges were folded inwards and dampened to form a bag for all that dried fruit. The centre having been pressed down, the whole cake was rolled out again to half an inch thickness. You could see the currants peeping through the pastry. Just as Cornish tin miners relied on Cornish pasties, Lancashire colliers took sadcake down the coal mines to form "good packing".

Chorley Cakes

4 oz (110 g) washed and dried currants
4 oz (110 g) lard or butter
8 oz (225 g) flour

Nowadays most people will prefer to use polyunsaturated fat, but the texture will differ.

Rub the fat into the flour lightly with the fingertips until the mixture resembles breadcrumbs. Bind this together with I tablespoon of iced water. Add the water carefully. Avoid using too much as this can make the pastry unmanageable. Roll out the pastry to a quarter inch thickness. Good pastry means keeping everything cool, so speed is important. Cut into four rounds about the size of a dinner plate. Place the currants centrally in these circles. Moisten the edges, fold over, press gently round the edges and roll out lightly until the currants show through the pastry. Place on a baking sheet in a moderate oven for 30 minutes. Sprinkle liberally with icing sugar.

Within the old boundaries Lancashire was robustly competitive. The dialect name for Chorley residents, "Chorley Currants", surely refers to the famous cake. In other villages e.g. Eagland Hill, "Club Cakes" were baked at gatherings such as Coffee Feasts. Ingredients were I 2 oz (350 g) plain flour, 8 oz (225 g) butter, 3 oz (75 g) sugar, but no fruit. These were also sprinkled .liberally with icing sugar.

Bury Simnel Cake

This is a traditional cake for Refreshment or Mothering Sunday. On Mothering Sunday, also known in Lancashire as Mid-Lent or Refreshment Sunday, all the young men and women who were employed in service in country houses or had to "live in" at large city shops, were allowed time to visit their homes, taking gifts of flowers to their mothers.

---

5 oz (150 g) butter
5 oz (150 g) sugar
2 eggs
8 oz (225 g) self raising flour
1 teaspoon mixed spice
8 oz (225 g) dried fruit
1 teaspoon ground cinnamon
4 oz (110 g) mixed peel
8 oz (225 g) almond paste or raw sugar marzipan
1 level tablespoon of apricot jam
milk to mix
egg to glaze

Cream together the butter and sugar and beat in the eggs one at a time. Sieve together the flour and spices and add the washed dried fruit and peel. Add sufficient milk to give a dropping consistency. Put the mixture into a greased and lined 8 inch (20 cm) cake tin and bake in a moderate oven for 80 minutes or until firm to touch.

When the cake is cold, brush the top with sieved jam and cover with a layer of almond paste. Score with a knife to make diamond patterns and crimp the edges. Brush with beaten egg and brown under the grill until golden.

Easter Cake

---

6 oz (175 g) soft margarine
5 oz (150 g) Muscavado sugar
8 oz (225 g) wholemeal flour
4 free range eggs
2 oz (50 g) ground almonds
¼ teaspoon cinnamon
4 oz (110 g) sultanas
4 oz (110 g) raisins
4oz (110 g) currants
grated rind of a lemon
1 tablespoon of milk
2 teaspoons baking powder
8 oz (225 g) packet of marzipan

Before you begin, set the oven at 160 C (325 F)

Cream the margarine and sugar until light and fluffy. Beat in the eggs one at a time. Sift in the flour and baking powder, then the ground almonds and cinnamon. Add all the fruits, cleaned and dried, and the lemon rind. Fold in all the ingredients with a metal spoon. Pour the mixture into an 8 inch (20 cm) diameter cake tin and smooth the top. Bake in the centre of the oven for two hours at 160 C (325 F). To test, insert a metal skewer into the cake centre; it should come out clean. If uncooked mixture is visible give the cake longer. To prevent over-browning place a sheet of moist greaseproof paper over the top of the cake. Leave it in the tin to cool. When the cake is cold brush the top with apricot jam. Roll out the marzipan on a lightly dusted surface of icing sugar and fit the round of marzipan onto the cake top. Any trimmings can be made into marzipan balls to decorate. These should be gently grilled on a baking sheet until golden brown.

Well into the 19th century, Easter Day was marked by "lifting", which commemorated the rising from the tomb. On Easter Monday the women were lifted into the air by the men and on Easter Tuesday the process was reversed.

Some of the inns had special chairs covered with satin and decked with ribbons for favoured guests to sit in and be "heaved". Christopher Sansom wrote ; "It was a boisterous day. What merry scenes! What humour in the faces of these Lancashire witches!"

Whitsuntide Walk Cake

8 oz (225 g) self raising flour
2 oz (50 g) porridge oats
4 oz (110 g) raisins
4 oz (110 g) sultanas
1 level teaspoon baking powder
3 eggs
2 oz (50 g) chopped walnuts
2 tablespoons of milk
6 oz (175 g) brown sugar
8 oz (225 g) soft margarine

Place all the ingredients except the fruit and nuts in a large bowl. Mix together thoroughly by beating well. Stir in the fruit and nuts. Turn the mixture into a greased and lined 11 inch (28 cm) by 7 inch (18 cm) cake tin. Level the top. Bake in a moderate oven. Turn the cake out when cool and stand it on a wire rack.

Frumenty, Jannocks and Throdkins

"A jannock of Lancashire" is mentioned in 1577 in the Shepherds' Play Cycle performed at Chester. Introduced by Flemish weavers, it came down to us as oatcake. Jannocks or throdkins were taken to the fields by agricultural workers who became ravenous from working in the open all day.

1 lb (450 g) coarse oatmeal
6 oz (175 g) lard
a good pinch of salt

After rubbing the lard into the oatmeal, mix with 2 tablespoons of water. Put in a shallow dish, place strips of bacon on top and cook in a slow oven. It could be eaten hot, or spread with butter and treacle for breakfast.

Frumenty, mentioned in the Bible, must be our oldest national dish. It was served on Mid-Lent Sunday and throughout the 12 days of Christmas. In the

1880s farmers' wives prepared it at "clipping time" (sheep shearing) and at the annual Harvest Home suppers and our ancestors enjoyed it at the Mediaeval Fairs of Merrie England.

An octogenarian farmer from Thornton-le-Fylde said: "To cree the wheat soak 12 hours and boil for 12 hours in milk, the liquid to be twice the amount of the wheat. Add a pat of butter, a dab of cream and as a special treat a cup full of rum." All the family took a hand in stirring the mass. A whole nutmeg was grated over it for "bite". Considered sustaining, it is praised today for its vitamin B content.

Grated real nutmeg is more spicy than the powdered variety and calls to mind a 13 year-old crippled boy of 150 years ago. Without arms or legs and orphaned, he scraped together an existence by selling nutmeg graters which were attached to his coat. He sold these for a penny each, sometimes three, sometimes none. In his words: "I often go without food." (Henry Mayhew's "London Labour and the London Poor")

Farmhouse Scones

8 oz (225 g) self raising flour

2 oz (50 g) margarine

2 oz (50 g) sugar

¼ pint (150 ml) milk

2 oz (50 g) sultanas

2 oz (50 g) chopped glace cherries

Pre-heat the oven to 200 C (400 F).

Sieve the flour into a mixing bowl and rub in the margarine with the fingertips until it resembles breadcrumbs. Stir in the sugar, sultanas and cherries. Add the milk and fashion with a knife or spatula into a dough. Knead it gently on a floured baking board and roll it out to 1 inch (2.5 cm) thickness. With a 3 inch (7.5 cm) pastry cutter make into rounds. Place on a baking sheet and cook for 20 minutes in a hot oven. These are very good served warm with butter and home-made jam.

M. Bay Ltd., Traditional Bakers, of High Street, Prescot, Merseyside, who are listed in the North West Fine Foods Guide to Quality Food and Drink, offer a full range of products and "very special Christmas Puddings".

Raspberry Jam

To spread on the scones, there's nothing better than home-made raspberry jam!

4½ lbs (2 kg) raspberries

3½ lbs (1.5 kg) sugar

2 tablespoons water

Clean and stalk the berries, rejecting any over-ripe fruit. Place in a preserving pan with the water and cook slowly over gentle heat till the Juices flow and the fruit softens. Add the warmed sugar and, once dissolved, bring quickly to the boil. Boil for only 8 minutes, thus retaining all natural flavours. Loganberries should be treated in the same way. Pot in warm, sterilised jars.

Treacle Loaf

---

8 oz (225 g) self raising flour

4 oz (110 g) dried fruit

2 oz (50 g) sugar

1 teaspoon baking powder

1 dessertspoon treacle

1 tablespoon golden syrup

5½ fl oz (160 ml) milk

1 egg

Mix the dry ingredients in a bowl. Melt the sugar, treacle and syrup together. Add to the dry ingredients and stir. Beat the egg and milk to make approximately 7½ fl oz (225 ml). Add to the mixture and stir well to make a soft consistency. Pour into a 2 lb (900 g) loaf tin and bake for I ½ hours at I 50 C (300 F).

Other versions of this traditional loaf, known as Lancashire Sticky Bread, were spread thickly with farm butter.

Ginger Fairings

8 oz (225 g) flour

1 teaspoon ginger

1 teaspoon mixed spice

2 teaspoons baking powder

½ teaspoon cinnamon

4 tablespoons Golden Syrup

4 oz (110 g) butter

3 oz (75 g) sugar

Sift the flour, spices and baking powder and mix well. Rub the butter in and add the sugar. Heat the syrup and pour this in also, working well into a dough. On a floured board roll into balls, flatten slightly and place on a greased baking sheet. Bake at 200 C (400 F) for under 20 minutes.

Market Place, Manchester, was a large area, two streets in length, where traders gathered in the early 19th century to shout their wares. The muffin lady came and the Chelsea bun man who, having found the buns so popular in London, had set up successfully in Manchester. James Robinson also cried his wares on Old Salford bridge, his bun tray round his neck. The Chelsea buns, covered with a white cloth, were kept warm by charcoal burning just below his tray. Nearby Mylngate had a communal bakers' oven.

Rich Clitheroe Parkin

1 lb (450 g) oatmeal

½ lb (225 g) lard

½ lb (225 g) butter

¼ lb (110 g) sugar

2 oz (50 g) ground ginger

½ lb (225 g) golden syrup

Melt the lard and butter together then mix with the syrup. Add the dry ingredients, mixing all thoroughly. Bake in a slow oven for two hours in a large, well-greased tin. Parkin was usually eaten at least three days old when it had softened.

A great novelty around 1910, Firth's Bakery used the aeroplane flying over Clitheroe to advertise their cakes fresh daily and their renowned parkin.

Date Ginger Parkin

8 oz (225 g) dates
1 lb (450 g) wholemeal flour
4 oz (110 g) syrup
4 oz (110 g) treacle
6 oz (175 g) margarine
6 teaspoons ground ginger
2 large free range eggs
½ pint (300 ml) water
2 teaspoons bicarbonate of soda
enough ginger wine to cover the dates

Cut the dates into small pieces and soak in ginger wine for 30 minutes. Drain. Place them in a pan with half of the water. Stir over low heat and add the margarine, syrup and treacle. Set aside when the margarine has melted. Sift the flour into a bowl with the ginger and bicarbonate of soda mixed together and add the beaten eggs. Add the melted ingredients from the pan and the rest of the cold water. Mix it well together and turn into a large, greased tin. Bake at 180 C (350 F) for 40 minutes. Allow to cool before attempting to turn the gingerbread out.

Praline Gateau

8 oz (225 g) unsalted butter
8 oz (225 g) caster sugar
9 oz (250 g) self raising flour
1 oz (25 g) ground almonds
4 eggs
1 tablespoon water

Cream the butter and sugar. Add the eggs one at a time, breaking them first into a cup and beating them well into the mixture. Add the sifted flour and the ground almonds then finally the water. Bake in a lined sandwich tin in a moderate oven for 1 hour 20 minutes.

Turn the cake out onto a cooling rack. While the cake is cooling, prepare the filling. The following are suitable ones – whichever you choose, simply cut the cake in two and spread the mixture between the two layers.

Chocolate Cream Filling

3 oz (75 g) butter
6 oz (175 g) icing sugar
3 oz (75 g) grated plain chocolate

Cream the butter, adding the icing sugar gradually. Gently melt the chocolate and beat into the creamed mixture.

Lemon Buttercream

4 oz (110 g) unsalted butter
4 tablespoons lemon curd
6 oz (175 g) sifted icing sugar

Beat the butter until soft and creamy, then gradually beat in the sifted icing sugar. Slowly beat in the lemon curd.

For coffee-flavoured buttercream, add 2 teaspoons of powdered coffee in place of the lemon curd.

Victoria Sponge Cake

4 oz (110 g) sifted self raising flour or sponge flour
4 oz (110 g) soft margarine
4 oz (110 g) caster sugar
2 eggs separated
1 tablespoon cold water

Cream together the margarine and sugar until light and creamy. Beat in the two egg yolks and the cold water.

In a separate bowl whisk the egg whites to a thick foam. Fold the flour into the mixtute. Gently fold in the whisked whites. Divide the mixture between two sandwich tins with loose bottoms. Level with a palette knife and bake in the oven at 180 C (350 F) until risen and golden brown. Cool on a wire tray and sandwich the two sponges together with raspberry jam. Dust with caster sugar.

Orange Drizzle Cake

Make a Victoria sponge cake mixture and add the grated rind of two oranges and the juice of one. Bake in a loaf tin and when nearly cold make slits in the top of the cake and "drizzle" in orange syrup.

To make this, mix the juice of one orange with 2 oz (50 g) sugar and heat gently until it forms into a syrupy liquid.

Strawberry and Cream Victoria

Victoria sponge cakes were great favourites of Queen Victoria. It is a good idea to make two in the strawberry season and decorate for a special occasion.

2 Victoria sponge cakes
1 lb (450 g) strawberries
¾ pint (450 ml) double cream
kirsch
flaked almonds

Split the cakes. Whip the cream. Save a few grand strawberries for decoration and mash the rest. Pour a little kirsch onto each sponge and sandwich the four together with the mashed fruit and whipped cream. Save a third of the cream and finish with a layer of mashed fruit on top. Spread the sides of the cake with cream and flaked nuts and decorate with the remaining strawberries, each cut in half. The rest of the cream can be piped on top with the last of the strawberries.

Real Cherry Cake

12 oz (350 g) self raising flour
6 oz (175 g) softened butter
6 oz (175 g) caster sugar
4 oz (110 g) washed, chopped and stoned cherries
grated rind of 1 lemon
¼ pint (150 ml) milk
2 beaten free range eggs
1 tablespoon lemon juice

Line a greased 2 lb (900 g) loaf tin with greaseproof paper.

Rub the butter into the flour until it resembles breadcrumbs. Stir in the sugar, chopped & stoned cherries and lemon rind, then add the beaten eggs, lemon juice and milk. Mix well and bake in a moderate oven until firm and golden.

Lemon Icing for the top of the cake

5 oz (150 g) icing sugar
1 dessert spoon lemon juice.

Mix together the icing sugar and lemon juice and spread evenly over the cake.

Lancashire was a county for clubs of all kinds which held processions and other activities. At Walton-le-Dale, birthdays were celebrated with a large cake at the "Autumn Tints" and "Spring Chicken" Clubs. At one 95th birthday party where portions of a large cake were passed round, there were nine nonagenarians present.

Cherry and Walnut Cake

6 oz (175 g) butter
6 oz (175 g) caster sugar
8 oz (225 g) flour
3 eggs
3 oz (75 g) glace cherries
1 level teaspoon baking powder
3 oz (75 g) chopped walnuts
rind and juice of 1 orange

Cream the butter and sugar, beat in the eggs and add the sifted flour and baking

The First Poulton Ranger Company held their second birthday party in 1932. Captain Gertrude
Jennings cuts the cake with Lieutenant Dorothy Hodgkinson on her right.

powder, cherries and walnuts, the rind and juice to be added last. Bake in a
moderate oven for about 1 ½ hours. This cake is further improved by a layer of
orange icing when cold. For this, add 2 oz (50 g) of icing sugar mixed with a tablespoon of freshly squeezed orange juice.

Cherry and Almond Cake

4 oz (110 g) margarine
4 oz (110 g) butter
8 oz (225 g) caster sugar
3 eggs
¼ teaspoon almond essence
4 oz (110 g) glace cherries, washed and halved
8 oz (225 g) plain flour
4 oz (110 g) ground almonds
1 level teaspoon baking powder
¼ teaspoon salt
1 tablespoon granulated sugar

Cream the butter, margarine and caster sugar until fluffy. Beat the eggs and almond essence together and gradually beat into a cream mixture. Stir in the cherries. Sieve the flour, ground almonds, baking powder and salt and fold in. Grease an 8 inch (20 cm) cake tin and line it with a double layer of greaseproof paper. Spoon the mixture into the tin and smooth the top. Sprinkle the cake with granulated sugar.

Cook in the centre of a pre-heated oven at 140 C (275 F) for 1½ hours and then, after 20 minutes, turn out the cake to finish cooling on a wire rack.

Carrot Cake

7 oz (200 g) brown sugar

5 oz (150 g) soft butter or soft margarine

2 large free range eggs

8 oz (225 g) finely grated carrot

7 oz (200 g) wholemeal flour

1 teaspoon baking powder

1 teaspoon cinnamon

4 oz (110 g) sultanas

1 teaspoon orange juice

1 teaspoon grated orange rind.

Pre-heat the oven to 180 C (350 F). Cream the butter or margarine and sugar, Beat in the eggs. Add the carrots and fold in the flour, baking powder and cinnamon. Mix in the sultanas, rind and Juice, Turn into a greased, lined 8 inch (20 cm) cake tin and bake for one hour.

An orange topping can be made by mixing:

4 oz (110 g) icing sugar

2 oz (50 g) butter

1 teaspoon orange juice

Beat all together and spread on the cake when cool. This cake does not keep.

Fruit Flapjack

---

5 oz (150 g) margarine

4 oz (110 g) brown sugar

8 oz (225 g) porridge oats

3 tablespoons golden syrup

2 oz (50 g) chopped dates

2 oz (50 g) chopped almonds

2 oz (50 g) glace cherries

2 oz (50 g) ready to eat dried apricots

Melt the margarine with the sugar and syrup in a large pan. Remove from heat and stir in the oats, apricots, dates, nuts and cherries. Place in a large, greased tin and press the mixture down well with a spatula. Bake at 180 C (350 F) for 25 minutes. Cut into portions whilst still hot in the tin.

Ginger Flapjack

As Lancashire was for centuries considered a fine oat-growing county it is not surprising that many oat-based recipes have survived. Flapjack was eaten in large quantities round farmhouse tables by the family and workers in the fields. Preparation for Ginger Flapjack was similar to that of fruit flapjack.

---

12 oz (350 g) butter

9 oz (250 g) brown sugar

18 oz (500 g) porridge oats

6 tablespoons golden syrup

3 teaspoons ground ginger

Lancashire and the Highlands of Scotland were oat cake country as far back as the 14th century. The Reivers baked them over camp fires using "gredils" which gave the name to "girdle" oat cakes.

In Lancashire, recruiting sergeants would fix an oat cake to the point of a sword to tempt volunteers. As oats were known as havers, the Regiment became known as the Havercake Lads.

Oat Biscuits

½ lb (225 g) rolled oats
¼ lb (110 g) granulated sugar
¼ lb flour
5 oz (150 g) margarine
1 egg

Put the dry ingredients into a bowl and rub in the margarine. Add the egg and mix well together. A little milk can be added if the mixture is stiff, but it should be fine enough to roll out to quarter inch thickness. Cut into 2 inch (5 cm) rounds and bake in a moderate oven for 10 minutes.

Uncle Jimmy's Treat, inspired by a local man James Charleston, was held annually on Easter Monday in Cuerden Park, Bamber Bridge. Commencing in a modest way in 1900, it grew so much that the road between the Hob Inn and the Pear Tree Hotel had to be closed for the precession to pass, led by "Uncle Jimmy" and Police Inspector Seth Clarkson. On passing through the Stag and Eagle gates of Mr. Tatton's estate each child was given an egg, an apple, an orange, a mug of coffee and a bun baked by local confectioner Mr. Byers.

Mrs. Moss's Almond Biscuits

8 oz (225 g) margarine
4 oz (110 g) icing sugar
8 oz (225 g) plain flour
2 oz (50 g) ground almonds
2 oz (50 g) cornflour
1 oz (25 g) sliced almonds
almond essence

Cream together the margarine, icing sugar and 10 drops of almond essence. Add all the rest and mix well. Form this dough into walnut-sized lumps. Flatten each lump and place on a greased baking tray with a slice of almond dipped in milk on top of each. Bake in a moderate oven until golden brown. This quantity makes 24 biscuits.

Martin's Ginger Honey Crunch

8 oz (225 g) margarine
2 oz (50 g) crushed cornflakes
10 oz (275 g) self raising flour
2 tablespoons of runny honey
4 oz (110 g) caster sugar
2 teaspoons ginger

Cream the margarine and sugar then add the other ingredients. Divide the mixture into small lumps, place on a greased baking tray and flatten each lump with a fork. Baked in a moderate oven for 10-15 minutes, this makes 36 biscuits.

The bell ringers of the Parish Church of St. Chad, Poulton-le-Fylde gathered recipes together in "Cooks in the Belfry" (now in its 5th edition) in aid of the church roof appeal. The £56,000 needed was eventually raised by public subscription. The ringers' biscuits in particular have since graced many a coffee morning and achieved quiet fame.

Grandma's Cream Horns

The horns can be made from flaky pastry. Bake them at 200 C (400 F) sufficiently long for them to puff up and brown, handle carefully and fill when cool. Flaky pastry is best bought frozen from the supermarket as it takes a skilled cook to accomplish perfection. Shape the horns around the handle of a large wooden spoon.

The cream filling is as follows:

4 oz (110 g) icing sugar
3 oz (75 g) butter
1 dessertspoon flour
1 dessertspoon boiling water
a few drops of vanilla essence

Mix all the ingredients to a smooth cream, adding more water if necessary.

Vegetarian Recipes

Vegetarian Bake

½ large onion, finely chopped

1 slice wholemeal breadcrumbs

2 teaspoons soy sauce

2 tomatoes skinned and chopped

1 teaspoon tomato purée

1 eating apple washed and grated

2 teaspoons ground almonds

1 teaspoon Herbes de Provence

black pepper and seasoning

Grease an oven-proof dish.

Mix all the ingredients together in a basin. Turn into the greased dish and smooth out with a spatula. Bake for 20 minutes at 220 C (425 F) until browned. For gravy, use half a vegetable stock cube. Serve with spinach.

Remove all the stalks from the spinach and wash free from grit in running cold water. Drain in a colander. Put into a pan with 2 tablespoons of boiling water and cook until tender – young spinach takes no more than 5 minutes. Turn into a colander and press out all the water, which may be saved to use in a stock pot. Chop the spinach finely. Return to the pan and add 1 oz (25 g) butter and a little pepper. Serve very hot.

Country Cakes, Time House, Lower Road, Knowle Green, near Preston, specialise in cakes suitable for vegetarians. Their home-made cakes from traditional recipes have a natural shelf life. There is a tea shop on the premises.

Organically grown vegetables on display at Ramsbottom Victuallers, "a unique emporium specialising in natural and artisan food and drink". The Village Restaurant, also run by Ros Hunter and Chris Johnson, uses mainly organic ingredients bought from local small-scale farms or imported from Italy. Possibly unique, this venture, started 15 years ago, has featured in the Good Food Guide since 1985 and attracted such personalities as Michael Meacher, Cyril Smith, Margaret Beckett and John Gummer. The wine shop has received acclaim as a veritable "Aladdin's Cave" of food and drink. Rosalind is one of the country's well-known lady chefs.

Savoury Nut Pie

---

1 lb (450 g) potatoes
8 oz (225 g) shelled nuts, finely ground
8 oz (225 g) onions
2 oz (50 g) butter
ground sea salt and peppercorns
fresh parsley and thyme
2 tablespoons milk

Boil the potatoes after peeling and mash them up in the milk. Add the seasoning. Slice the onions finely and fry them gently in the butter. Mix them with the mashed potatoes then put in the nuts and chopped herbs. Bind with the milk. Place in a well-buttered dish and scatter small nuts of butter on top. Bake in a moderate oven for 15 minutes.

Meatless Shepherd's Pie

Many people these days favour vegetarian meals but it is important to gain protein from another source. W. Jordan Ltd., who have been milling wholemeal flour and wheatgerm since 1855, recommend this recipe, which also provides vitamins B1, B6, E and folic acid. Versatile wheatgerm can be used in dozens of ways. Try adding a tablespoon of it to soups and stews. It's also good and nourishing in porridge.

---

5 oz (150 g) lentils

1 large onion skinned and chopped

3 cloves garlic, crushed

2 teaspoons mixed herbs

salt and pepper to taste

1¼ lbs (550 g) potatoes peeled and chopped into large, even pieces

1½ oz (40 g) wheatgerm

1 tablespoon semi-skimmed milk

1½ oz (40 g) margarine

1 tin chopped tomatoes

4 oz (110 g) courgettes, sliced

5 oz (150 g) mixed peppers, roughly chopped

3 tablespoons tomato purée

1 tablespoon chopped fresh parsley

parsley to garnish

Wash the lentils thoroughly and put into a saucepan with the garlic, onion, herbs and pepper. Cover with 1½ pints (900 ml) water. Bring to the boil, cover and simmer for 12 minutes. Drain off all the cooking liquid and mash the lentils. Add the tomatoes, tomato purée, courgettes, Jordan's Wheat Germ and the peppers. Warm gently for 5 minutes then add the parsley. Meanwhile, cook the potatoes in boiling water for 15 minutes. Drain and mash with ½ oz (15 g) margarine, 1 tablespoon milk and the seasoning. Pile the mashed potato on top of the lentil mixture. Pattern the top with a fork and dot with the remaining margarine. Place under the grill for 15 minutes until browned.

Mr. Edwin Hall and daughter Jessie of Crumpsall. When George Bernard Shaw was preaching the gospel of vegetarianism he had but a small, select band of adherents, but the healthy Halls and Howarths continued down the generations to cook vegetarian meals.

Nut Roast

8 oz (225 g) shelled nuts

1 medium sized onion

6 oz (175 g) breadcrumbs

1 dessertspoon tomato sauce

1 oz (25 g) butter

1 cup mashed potatoes

1 egg

2 tablespoons vegetable stock

salt and pepper to taste

Chop the nuts finely and beat up the butter in a frying pan. Grate the onion and put it, with the nuts, into the pan. Fry for 3 minutes. Stir in the breadcrumbs, seasoning and tomato sauce. Add the beaten egg, stock and mashed potato. Mix all well together and turn into a buttered Pyrex dish. Bake until brown in a moderate oven for 25 minutes. Thinly sliced, ripe tomatoes are good with hot nut roast.

Vegetarian Paté

8 oz (225 g) grated carrots

¼ pint (150 ml) orange juice

8 oz (225 g) cream cheese

3 eggs

3 oz (75 g) chopped hazelnuts

1 teaspoon Mediterranean herbs

3 oz (75 g) dried apricots

3 oz (75 g) breadcrumbs

Cook the carrots in the orange juice for 20 minutes. Beat all the ingredients together. Place in a greaseproof paper-lined loaf tin topped with oiled foil. Stand the tin in a dish of hot water and bake for 45-50 minutes. The pate should be firm to the touch. Allow it to cool before removing from the tin. New potatoes dripping in butter and well-chopped fresh chives can make this into a satisfying meal.

The Woods at Great Harwood c.1920 where, according to reports from old aunts and uncles, hazelnuts, also known as filberts, could be found. They were collected in baskets in the autumn to be eaten on the spot or kept salted for use at Christmas when they were gently roasted.

Cheese and Potato Cake

On the main road through Heywood, a favourite stopping place around the turn of the 19th century was The Star, an inn with good stabling and homely fare. Cheese potato cake was popular with the many carters *en route* to busy Lancashire towns.

1½ lbs (675 g) potatoes
3 oz (75 g) butter
4 oz (110 g) grated Lancashire cheese
1 large onion, peeled and finely chopped

Scrub the potatoes then boil them for 10 minutes. Drain and cool, then peel. When completely cooled, grate the potatoes into a bowl. Melt 1 oz (25 g) butter in a non-stick pan and gently fry the onion for 5 minutes until soft. Remove from the pan and mix in with the grated potato. Add the remaining butter to the pan and melt.

Form the potato and onion into a cake and fry it gently for 7 minutes until golden brown. Invert it onto a plate. Replace in the pan and fry the other side likewise. Sprinkle the potato cake with cheese and place under the grill until bubbling.

Grandma Singleton's award-winning Lancashire cheese is produced at Singleton's Dairy Ltd., Mill Farm, Longridge. This is a fourth generation family business producing a wide range of cheeses.

Courgette Pasta for two

2 onions
1 tablespoon olive oil
1 clove of garlic, crushed
1 lb (450 g) courgettes
3 large ripe tomatoes
pinch of basil
4 oz (110 g) pasta shells
1 pint (600 ml) chicken stock
2 heaped teaspoons grated cheese

In a large, heavy pan soften the 2 sliced onions in a tablespoon of olive oil with the garlic.

Early Morning Market Delivery. Mr. J.A. Tatham of Tarleton was a well-known supplier of locally grown vegetables. Pictured 80 years ago, his brother is bringing market produce to Merseyside. Celery, carrots, potatoes, watercress and tomatoes were freshly gathered, the good earth still upon them. Grapes were packed in barrels of cork crumbs, oranges in tall, slatted, wooden boxes.

Wash, peel, top and tail the courgettes. Dice them and put them in the pan with the basil and the 3 chopped and peeled tomatoes and cover them with water. Bring to the boil then simmer uncovered until the water has evaporated. In lightly salted water, part-cook the pasta shells then place them in a pan with the chicken stock and complete the cooking until "al dente" – meaning well done but still firm. Stir in the grated cheese and serve hot.

Cauliflower Cheese

---

1 small cauliflower
2 oz (50 g) cheese
1 oz (25 g) butter
1 teaspoon chopped parsley
1 tablespoon milk
ground sea salt and pepper
pinch of Herbes de Provence

Boil the cauliflower until just tender. Remove the white part and beat it with a fork. Season and add the herbs, the finely grated cheese and the milk. Put the mixture in an ovenproof dish and sprinkle a little grated cheese on top.

Cut up the butter and scatter on top of this, then brown in a moderate oven. Garnish with parsley. For this dish I used Mrs. Kirkham's organic Lancashire cheese, which has recently been praised in London.

Parsnip Balls

---

4 medium sized parsnips

½ pint (300 ml) stock

2 oz (50 g) shelled nuts

¼ pint (150 ml) water

½ oz (15 g) butter

4 tablespoons breadcrumbs

1 egg

1 tablespoon flour

ground sea salt and pepper

Mince the nuts. Prepare the parsnips and cut them up. Cook in the stock until tender, adding more water if necessary. Season and mash until smooth. Form them into balls, using a floured board. When cold, dip them into the beaten egg and coat them with nuts and breadcrumbs. Place in a well-greased tin and brown in a hot oven.

Courgettes and Tomatoes

Fry some peeled, sliced garlic cloves in 3 tablespoons of virgin olive oil. Virgin oil from the first pressing of the olives has the most delicate flavour. Young courgettes need no peeling. Cut them into chunks and, having discarded the garlic cloves, toss into the oil with 4 sliced, sun-ripened tomatoes. Sprinkle with grated cheese, put in a ovenproof dish and bake in a moderate oven for 40 minutes.

Lancastrians who have visited the Mediterranean islands have formed a taste for food cooked in the finest olive oil as it is delicious, easily digested and cholesterol-free. Many olive trees planted in Biblical times still bear fruit and some in Sicily are venerated by the peasants.

The Seven Stars, Manchester, the oldest licensed house in Great Britain, "licensed for 504 years". Next to this was the five-storey building of a well-known cheese factor, Thomas Tallis & Co. Ltd. Ploughman's Lunches would no doubt be available at the Seven Stars Hotel.

Celery Cream

1 good stick of celery (in autumn, Ormskirk celery is excellent)

2 rashers fatty bacon

1 large onion

1 carrot

2 tablespoons cream

1 pint (600 ml) skimmed milk

ground sea salt and pepper

Remove the outer leaves from the celery and cut off the green tops. Wash the white celery thoroughly and cut into short lengths. Place these in boiling water and cook for 8 minutes. Drain and lay the celery in cold water. Cut the bacon finely and put in a cast-iron casserole. Add the onion and carrot, peeled and sliced into rings. Drain the cold water from the celery and put it in the casserole. Cover with the milk and simmer until the celery is cooked through. Drain off the liquid and boil it down to ½ pint (300 ml) then slowly add the cream and seasoning. Pour this sauce over the celery and serve.

Buttered Cheesy Cabbage

1 lb (450 g) Spring cabbage, washed, stalks removed,
shredded
2 oz (50 g) butter
2 oz (50 g) Cheddar cheese

Grate the cheese. Melt the butter in a warm casserole and stir in half a cup of boiling water. Make layers of cabbage and shredded cheese, finishing with cheese. Cover the casserole with a lid or foil and bake for 30 minutes in a moderate oven,

> The Eagle and Child, Bispham Green near Parbold, Lancashire Dining Pub of the Year in 1998, specialises in local food: lamb from Haigh Hall, Wigan; chicken and duck from Goosnargh; vegetables from the fertile Lancashire Plain.

Spring Sunshine Salad

12 oz (350 g) new potatoes scrubbed and quartered
½ cucumber peeled, cut in half and sliced
4 ripe tomatoes, quartered
1 oz (25 g) olives, pitted and halved
3 oz (75 g) diced Lancashire cheese
1 small onion, sliced thinly
1 tablespoon freshly chopped mint

The Dressing

3 tablespoons cold-pressed virgin olive oil
1 clove garlic crushed
1 tablespoon cider vinegar
ground sea salt
freshly ground black pepper

Simmer the potatoes for 15 minutes until tender. Drain and cool. Combine the potatoes with all the other salad ingredients. Put the dressing ingredients in a screw-topped jar and shake well. Pour over the tossed salad.

Recipes from Far & Wide

With so many travelling abroad for their holidays, here are some recipes to remind Lancashire folk – and others – of Greece, Italy and further afield.

Moussaka

3 oz (75 g) butter
2 aubergines
2 large onions sliced
2 tablespoons virgin olive oil
¼ pint (150 ml) water
1 lb (450 g) minced lamb
knob of butter
1 tablespoon tomato purée
freshly ground salt

Cut the aubergines into thin slices. Sprinkle with ground sea salt lightly and leave for half an hour, then rinse and drain them. Fry quickly in butter and olive oil until golden. Remove from the pan and put aside. Fry the onions in the remaining butter and oil until pale gold. Add the minced meat and cook until it browns, then put in the water and tomato purée and stir well. Line the bottom of a square oven-proof dish with half of the slices of aubergine. Cover with the meat mixture and the onions. Arrange the rest of the aubergines on top.

The Cheese Sauce

½ oz (15 g) cornflour
2 oz (50 g) grated mild Lancashire cheese
½ pint (300 ml) milk
small knob of butter
1 beaten egg

Mix the cornflour to a smooth paste with a little of the milk. Warm the remainder of the milk in a pan. Pour the paste onto the milk and gradually mix in well. Cook, stirring until the sauce thickens and boils. Simmer for 5 minutes to ensure that the cornflour cooks. Stir in the knob of butter. Remove from heat. Beat the egg into the sauce and, having re-heated, pour it over the Moussaka. Sprinkle on the grated cheese and bake at 180 C (350 F) for one hour.

Chicken Mexicana

1 large tomato
2 garlic cloves
2 medium-sized onions
3oz (75g) well chopped walnuts
1 green and 1 red pepper
2 tablespoons virgin olive oil
4 skinned and boned chicken breasts
½ pint (300 ml) chicken stock
2 tablespoons white wine
3 oz (75g) cheddar cheese
sea salt

Pour boiling water over the tomato, leave for four minutes then make cuts in the skin when cool. It will peel easily. Chop and set aside.

Peel and chop the onions. Pureé them in a food processor along with the crushed garlic cloves and walnuts.

Cut the peppers in half and remove the seeds and pith. Cut them into small pieces.

Heat the oil in a big pan and fry the chicken breasts for 6 minutes. Remove from the pan. Add tomato, peppers and pureé to the pan and pour in the stock. Bring to the boil, seasoning with the sea salt and wine.

Having reduced the heat, put in the chicken. Replace pan lid. Turn off the heat and wait until the cheese has melted.

Serve with a crisp salad of lettuce and watercress.

Pork Stir Fry

8 oz (225 g) lean pork steaks
8 oz (225 g) green vegetables (e.g. courgettes, French beans)
1 crushed clove of garlic
5 tablespoons thinned tomato sauce

Just before you start with this dish, prepare the rice. Basmati is best, though a little more expensive. For four people, add a cup of rice and two cups of water to a large saucepan. Bring to the boil then leave to simmer over a low heat for

10 minutes. Remove from the heat and leave for a further 10 minutes and you will have perfect boiled rice.

While that is happening, cut the meat and vegetables into thin strips. In a wok or deep frying pan, dry fry the meat for 3 minutes. Add the vegetables and garlic and cook for 2-3 minutes. Pour in the thinned sauce and bring to the boil. Serve hot with rice.

A quick Lamb Stir Fry can be made in much the same way using peppers, mange-tout and a salsa sauce, finishing with a sprinkling of cheese. Mozzarella or mature Cheddar is recommended.

Beef Curry

Cooked on a large scale from Aunt Kate's recipe, whenever meat was available in wartime this curry made a welcome change from Welsh Rarebit (mustard-flavoured cheese on toast). Any left over was warmed up next day and declared tastier than ever, but it is warned that this is not a practice to be recommended.

¾ pint (450 ml) beef stock

2 lbs (900 g) stewing steak cubed

2 oz (50 g) sultanas

2 large onions skinned and chopped

juice of ½ lemon

1 large cooking apple chopped

1½ oz (35 g) flour

1 level tablespoon curry powder

2 tablespoons chutney

4 tomatoes skinned and puréed

Place the steak, tomatoes, apple, sultanas, and half of the beef stock in a large terracotta casserole. In the rest of the stock gently cook the onions and curry powder and stir in the flour. After 10 minutes add this to the main casserole. With the lid on, allow the curry to cook out slowly for 2-3 hours.

Chicken Curry

4 skinned chicken breasts
1 tablespoon flour
salt and black pepper
1 mango
½ fresh pineapple
2 tablespoons olive oil
3 teaspoons curry powder
7½ fl oz (225 ml) chicken stock
¼ pint (150 ml) natural yoghurt
2 tablespoons grated coconut
1 small portion of stem ginger, chopped

Cut the chicken into strips and toss these into the seasoned flour. Chop the mango flesh with the cored, peeled pineapple and add the ginger. Fry the strips of chicken in oil for 5 minutes until browned. Remove from the pan and set aside. Fry the mixed fruits and the curry powder, stirring for 2 minutes. Add the

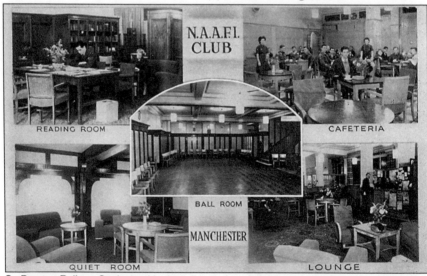

On Preston Railway Station to this day a brass plate dating back to the first World War is kept highly polished. It reads: "This Refreshment Room was by permission of the Lancashire and Yorkshire and London and North Western Railways occupied from August 19th 1915 to November 11th 1919 by the Preston Station Sailors and Soldiers Free Buffet Association of Voluntary Workers who supplied three and a quarter millions of sailors and soldiers who passed through this station, with refreshments and comforts."

chicken stock and bring to the boil, then lower the heat and simmer for 5 minutes.

Return the chicken to the pan and stir in the yoghurt, simmering on for 5 minutes. Finally, sprinkle the coconut over all and serve with mango chutney, basmati rice and poppadums.

Laila's Fine Foods, 19 Arkwright Court, Blackpool and Fylde Industrial Estate, Peel, supply Eastern and Western dishes, using only the freshest ingredients.

Lamb Kebabs

Cube 1 lb (450 g) lean lamb loin or leg steaks.

The Marinade

3 tablespoons tomato ketchup
2 tablespoons red wine vinegar
1 tablespoon virgin olive oil
1 tablespoon fresh, chopped basil
sea salt and black pepper
1 tablespoon fresh, chopped thyme

In a large bowl mix together all the marinade ingredients plus seasoning. Add the meat, making sure it is evenly coated. Leave overnight in the refrigerator. Thread the cubes of lamb onto skewers. If wooden skewers are used they should be soaked in water before use. Cook under the grill or barbecue over charcoal for 20 minutes, turning occasionally. A rice salad with cooked green beans can be served with the kebabs.

Children's Favourites

Lamb Burgers for Four

1 chopped onion
1 crushed clove of garlic
½ oz (15 g) butter
1 lb (450 g) minced lamb, fat removed
1 beaten egg
1 tablespoon chopped parsley
4 rashers streaky bacon

Fry the onion and garlic in the butter. Put the lamb in a bowl, add the onion and garlic, then the beaten egg, mixing well. Cut the bacon into 8 strips and divide the mixture in the bowl into 8 portions. Shape into burgers and wrap the bacon around each. Cook both sides of each burger under a hot grill until brown and well-cooked.

Shepherd's Pie

1 medium onion, chopped
1 lb (450 g) minced lamb or beef, fat removed
2 tablespoons flour
½ pint (360 ml) lamb or beef stock
1 tablespoon tomato purée
½ teaspoon scattered Herbes de Provence
1 oz (25 g) butter
1½ lbs (675 g) potatoes
3 tablespoons fresh milk
salt and freshly ground pepper

Dry fry the meat in a heavy pan until browned. Add the onion and cook for 5 minutes. Add the flour, stirring as you gradually blend in the stock and tomato purée, the herbs and seasoning. Stir until the mixture thickens and boils, then cover and simmer for 30 minutes. Put the mince into an ovenproof dish. Wash and peel the potatoes and cook them for 20 minutes or until tender. Drain, then mash them with butter and milk. Spread the potato over the mixture, using a fork, and bake at 190 C (375 F) for an hour.

Chefs James and Joseph make marmalade. With apples in the orchard in plenty and blackberries in their large garden, the little boys also have a hand in jelly making when Autumn comes.

Carrots and Turnips in Hollandaise Sauce

1 lb (450 g) young carrots
1 lb (450 g) turnips

Scrape and peel the carrots and turnips and cook them separately until tender.

The Sauce

1 oz (25 g) butter
1 oz (25 g) flour
½ pint (300 ml) milk
yolk of 1 egg
juice of ½ lemon

Melt the butter in a saucepan over gentle heat but do not allow to boil, then very gradually stir in the flour, using a wooden spoon. To keep the mixture smooth add the flour a little at a time until it forms a white roux. Add the milk very slowly, stirring well all the time over gentle heat. Stir until it boils then simmer for 10 minutes so that the flour is cooked. A richer white sauce can be made by adding 1 tablespoon of cream.

Beat the egg yolk and stir this into the white sauce for 3 minutes but do not let the sauce boil. Drip in the lemon juice gradually. Toss the carrots and turnips into the sauce and serve.

Toad in the Hole

1 oz (25 g) butter
1 lb (450 g) sausages
4 oz (110 g) flour
1 egg
½ pint (300 ml) fresh milk

Place the butter and sausages in a 10 inch (25.5 cm) x 12 inch (30.5 cm) roasting tin and cook at 220 C (425 F) for 10 minutes. Meanwhile sift the flour into a bowl and break in the egg centrally. Gradually add half the milk, beating well to keep the mixture smooth. Pour the batter into the roasting tin and bake for 40-45 minutes until the batter is golden and risen. You may need to pour off some of the sausage fat before adding the batter.

DONKEYS ON THE SANDS, MORECAMBE.   N.º 464.

Morecambe c.1920 during Wakes Weeks, which originally fell between Spring and Summer harvests. These patient donkeys were often overworked until 1942 when a donkey charter banned adult riders and stipulated a rest period. Carrot cake for the donkeys was one small boy's bright idea.

Batter for Shrimps or for Apple Fritters

This is a 1921 recipe. If you intend to use it to coat shrimps, two grinds of sea salt will add the required seasoning.

---

1 cup of flour

½ teaspoon baking powder

1 egg

½ cup of milk

Sift the dry ingredients. Add the beaten egg with the milk and beat the batter well until it is smooth,

If apple fritters are for a party of 10 children, then 2 lbs (900 g) of Bramley apples will be needed and double the quantity of batter. Peel, core and slice the fruit about ½ inch (1 cm) thick. Coat each side with batter. Drop the slices into hot olive oil. Fry for 1 minute and turn, allowing another 4 minutes. Drain well and allow to cool as the apple will emerge very hot.

The Lancashire Branch of the Children's Home and Orphanage at Edgworth had a Model Bakery. The men are making cottage loaves and tin loaves, some of which would be used for bread and butter pudding for the orphans.

Bread and Butter Pudding from Oswaldtwistle

8 slices of buttered bread, thin and crustless

3 oz (75 g) soft brown sugar

4 oz (110 g) stoned sultanas

1 pint (600 ml) milk

2 free range eggs

grated rind of 1 lemon

grated nutmeg

Spread butter over the bottom and sides of a 2 pint (1 200 ml) dish and sprinkle with sugar. Cut the buttered bread into small squares. Make alternate layers with bread, sultanas, lemon rind and sugar, finishing with a layer of bread. Sprinkle the top with grated nutmeg and sugar. Beat the eggs and add the milk. Pour this over the pudding and let soak for 30 minutes. Cook in a moderate oven until crisp and brown on top.

Shortbread was always a favourite with children and it was one of the most popular cakes baked by W. & M. Gibson, Confectioners. The procession in 1946 passes their premises, the oldest-established bakery in Poulton-le-Fylde, on its way to Lower Green where traditionally May Day dancing was held. Once the chief festivity of the year, when oxen drew the Maypole to the Green and a King and Queen of May were elected, Poulton Festival revives the ceremony annually.

Shortbread

4 oz (110 g) softened butter

2 oz (50 g) caster sugar

5 oz (150 g) flour

Cream the butter and sugar till fluffy. Stir in the flour and with fingertips gently press the mixture together and place in a buttered sandwich tin. Press flat and prick all over. Bake for 40 minutes at 160 C (325 F). The shortbread should not brown but be a pale golden colour. Leave in the tin and after cutting into portions dredge more caster sugar over the shortbread.

Ormskirk Brandy Snaps

---
2 oz (50 g) plain flour

3 oz (75 g) caster sugar

3 oz (75 g) golden syrup

1 teaspoon brandy

2 oz (50 g) best butter

1 teaspoon ground ginger

Grease 2 baking sheets. Sift the flour and ginger. Gently melt the butter, sugar and golden syrup in a saucepan. Take off the heat and stir in all the other ingredients. Place teaspoonfuls of the mixture on the baking sheets, allowing room for them to spread. Bake for 10 minutes at 180 C (350 F) at the top of the oven until golden brown. Allow to cool slightly then loosen the areas of the spreading mixture and whilst malleable, curl them round the greased handle of a wooden spoon. The brandy snaps will set in the traditional curled shape.

From time immemorial Ormskirk Market stalls displayed vegetables freshly dug early that morning, freshly picked local fruit in season, traditional gingerbread and brandy snaps, locally produced butter and cheese and home-made jams and treacle toffee. It was a place that children loved.

Strawberry Ice Cream

---
1 lb (450 g) puréed strawberries

1 pint (600 ml) fresh double cream

4 oz (110 g) sifted icing sugar

2 teaspoons vanilla essence

4 tablespoons fresh milk

Turn the freezer to "fast freeze" button 1 hour before placing ice cream in the freezer.

Pour the cream and milk into a chilled bowl and beat both together. Stir in the icing sugar and vanilla essence. Stir in the puréed strawberres. Pour into a freezer container and freeze for 45 minutes. Transfer to a chilled bowl, beat with a fork and stir gently until smooth. Return to another freezer container and freeze for 2 hours or until firm.

Enjoying those universal favourites strawberry and blackcurrant ice cream on a hot day in August 1993 during school holidays. Patrick, Eleanor and Eddie had just walked three miles for their treat.

Cardinal Sauce

Make the sauce when strawberries are in season to pour over vanilla ice cream. Wash 8 oz (225 g) of strawberries and 8 oz (225 g) of raspberries. Liquidise in a blender and rub through a sieve. Sweeten the sauce to taste. This makes a welcome Christmas treat for children.

Egg Custard

---

3 eggs

1 oz (25 g) sugar

1 pint (600 ml) milk

Beat the eggs. Boil the milk and add it gradually to the beaten eggs. Stir in the sugar. Turn the mixture into a jug and stand the jug in a saucepan of boiling water placed over gentle heat. Stir until the custard is thick and creamy.

Blackcurrant Mousse

---

1 lb (450 g) of blackcurrants

4 oz (110 g) of caster sugar

½ oz (15 g) of powdered gelatine

whites of 2 large free-range eggs

8 tablespoons water

Cook the blackcurrants in 5 tablespoons of water over low heat until tender. Strain into a basin and stir the sugar into the juice. In another basin put 3 tablespoons of water and sprinkle in the gelatine. Leave for 5 minutes. To ensure the gelatine is well-dissolved stand it in a basin of warm water and stir continuously. Pour this slowly into the blackcurrant juice, whisking at the same time. Later place the cooled basin of juice in the fridge until it has thickened and is on the point of setting. Fold in the beaten egg whites. Put into individual glasses and place back in the fridge until set. Children like sponge finger biscuits with this sweet.

Dad's Treacle Toffee

This toffee was obligatory on Bonfire Night, November 5th. Other people called it Plot Toffee in memory of Guy Fawkes and the Gunpowder Plot.

---

1 lb (450 g) demerara sugar

8 oz (225 g) treacle

12 oz (350 g) unsalted butter

1 small tub – 145 ml (5 oz) – of single cream

2 tablespoons water

pinch of cream of tartar

Put the water into a pan, add the sugar, treacle and a little butter. Heat very slowly so as not to burn the mixture. Thinly slice the rest of the butter and add gradually with the cream of tartar. Bring to the boil. Test a small quantity by dropping it into cold water. If it forms into a hard lump it is ready. Allow to cool down, but before it sets stir in the cream and pour the toffee into a well-greased tin. It sets very quickly and can be broken with a small toffee hammer before putting pieces in screws of greaseproof paper.

Nut Butter Toffee

4 oz (110 g) butter
8 oz (225 g) sugar
2 tablespoons vinegar
3 tablespoons golden syrup
4 oz (110 g) blanched almonds

Melt the butter in a thick pan over low heat. Add the sugar, syrup and vinegar and stir well. Bring to the boil, still stirring until the mixture becomes pale brown. Test a drop in a basin of cold water to see if it hardens. Spread almonds evenly over the base of a shallow bowl and pour the mixture over it. Leave to cool and set.

Before moving to Radcliffe, Hall Brothers' Toffee Works covered a considerable area in Whitefield. As the Grammar School boys and girls got off the train, ambrosial minty scents assailed their nostrils. Rowland Hall (nicknamed "Toffee" Hall) was the first Whitefield man to fly for pleasure – on Saturday afternoons in the 1930s he would fly over the grounds of Stand and Whitefield Cricket Club where Robert Hall, President of the Club, held the record with four hat tricks.

Simple Cottage Candy

1 lb (450 g) soft brown sugar
4 oz (110 g) unsalted butter
4 tablespoons milk

Melt the ingredients over low heat then boil gently until the mixture thickens. Remove from heat and beat until creamy. Pour into a buttered tray and mark into small squares whilst still warm.

Peppermint Creams

8 oz (225 g) sieved icing sugar
1 teaspoon cream
white of 1 egg
a few drops of peppermint oil

Beat the egg white and add the sugar, cream and flavouring. Beat all with a wooden spoon and then work well with the flat of the hand until smooth. Roll gently on a board dusted with icing sugar and cut out shapes. Leave to dry overnight in a cool larder,

Susan's Farmhouse Fudge, Gregson Farm, Samlesbury is a family business producing quality home-made fudge, toffee, chocolate animals and truffles. With no artificial preservatives they are "a taste of the good old days".

Blackberry and Apple Jam

2¼ lbs (1 kg) cooking apples

4½ lbs (2 kg) ripe blackberries

1 pint (600 ml) water

Allow 1 lb (450 g) sugar to each pint (600 ml) of prepared fruit.

Peel core and quarter the apples. Put them in a jar and place this in a preserving pan half full of cold water. Heat gradually and allow to boil until the apples in the jar are soft.

Put the blackberries in a pan with a pint (600 ml) of water and simmer until a pulp is formed. Rub the pulp through a fine sieve, which will eliminate all the seeds. Mix this with the apples. Measure the fruit and put it into the preserving pan, allowing I lb (450 g) of sugar to every pint (600 ml). Simmer until a set is achieved. Children love this jam as it is sweet and seedless.

Rowanberry Jelly

3 lbs (2.5 kg) rowanberries

3 lbs (2.5 kg) cooking apples

1 lb (450 g) sugar to each pint (600 ml) of juice

Wash the berries and remove the stalks. Wash and cut up the apples but do not core or peel.

In separate pans cover the fruits with cold water. Stew until the apples are soft and colour has flowed deeply red from the rowanberries. Drain off the juices without pressing the fruits. Measure the combined juices, allowing I lb (450 g) sugar to every pint (600 ml). Boil until a set is achieved, testing as you go to avoid over-boiling which would produce a stiff jelly.

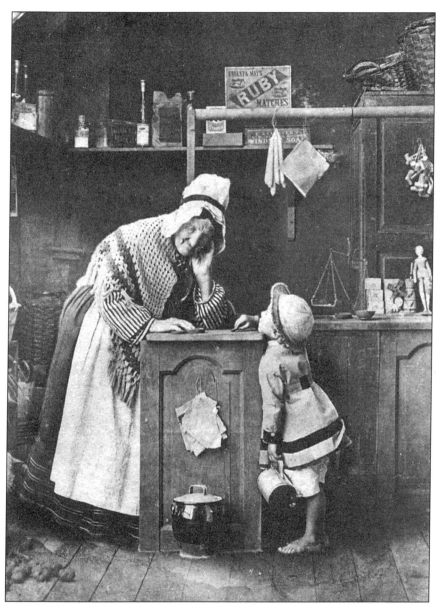

"A pennyworth of butter drops, please!" Freddy Lyth's stall on Haslingden Market used to amaze children as he took bubbly toffee out of its pan, slapped it down on a powdered tray, rolled it, pulled it and flung it onto a hook attached to his stall. Mouths wide open, they waited for the "ends" when Freddy cut up the toffee like seaside rock. All this was in tune with the celery man's calls from Deardengate. "Penny, ha'penny, tuppence, tuppence ha'penny" as he auctioned off the last of his celery hearts.

Whinberry and Rhubarb Jelly

This is a very old recipe from Stacksteads near Bacup. At one time, whinberries grew in profusion on the moors above the Rossendale Valley.

2 lbs (900 g) rhubarb
8 oz (225 g) whinberries
sugar

Dry and peel the rhubarb and cut into 1 inch (2.5 cm) lengths. Pick over the whinberries for stalks and twigs, then whip the fruit gently, taking care not to bruise it. Just cover the rhubarb with cold water and cook until mushy. Add the whinberries and cook until all is well mixed to a lovely deep purple. To every pint (600 ml) of fruit add 1 lb (450 g) of warm sugar. Dissolve and boil until setting point is reached (test a spoonful on a cold plate). Allow to cool then put into warm jars and cover each with wax discs and well-fixed jam pot covers. Label.

Seasoners Fine Foods Ltd., 69 Acorn Centre off Barry Street, Derker, Oldham, supply a fine range of pickles, preserves and sauces, using traditional methods and the freshest of ingredients.

Chocolate Cake

4 oz (110 g) sugar
6 oz (175 g) flour
4 oz (110 g) margarine
2 well-beaten eggs
4 oz (110 g) golden syrup
2 oz (500 g) drinking chocolate
2 oz (50 g) dark chocolate
½ teaspoon instant coffee

In a pan, warm

¼ pint (150 ml) milk
½ teaspoon bicarbonate of soda

To the softened margarine add the syrup, sugar, flour, drinking chocolate and instant coffee. Mix in the 2 well-beaten eggs and lastly put in the cooled milk and bicarbonate of soda.

Place the mixture in two loose-bottomed tins and bake for 25 minutes at 190 C (375 F). When cool, the 2 cakes can be sandwiched together with the 2 oz (50 g) melted dark chocolate.

Baked Apple Dumplings

As children, we loved these apple dumplings with real egg custard

1 lb (450 g) self raising flour
8 oz (225 g) margarine
4 oz (110 g) lard
4 medium-sized cooking apples
milk to mix
a mixed cupful of creamed butter, sugar and raisins

Sift the flour. Rub in the margarine and lard lightly with fingertips and add a little milk gradually to form a dough. Avoid a sticky consistency. Roll out the pastry on a floured board and cut into rounds the size of a tea plate. Peel the apples and remove every scrap of core. Fill the centres of the apples with creamed butter, sugar and raisins; redcurrant jelly and honey are alternative fillings.

Place an apple on each round of the pastry, draw up the pastry to the centre, wet the edges with cold water and press them onto the apples. Place the dumplings in a ovenproof dish, brush over with milk and bake in a moderate oven for 30 minutes.

Chefs' Specials

Lack of space precludes mention of all the excellent Lancashire inns, hotels and restaurants run by experienced chefs, but here is a small selection:

Paul Heathcote

Paul has been nominated "Chef of the Year", one of "The Great Chefs of the World" and owner of "One of the best restaurants of the world". His first book, "Rhubarb and Black Pudding", encapsulating one Michelin-starred year in his glittering career, echoes his Lancashire roots. Paul is renowned for uncompromising excellence and, as we chatted in his Longridge restaurant, I was quietly delighted to learn that imagination is as important to him as expertise. A keen cricketer, on Saturday afternoons he exchanges his white chef's coat for his cricketing whites, to open the bowling for his local team. Chipping. At this point; thoughts of culinary excellence give way to his immediate objective to see off the opposing openers with his fast/medium

Paul with Catherine

swingers and, as a middle order batsman, to round off the day with a match-winning innings.

Black Pudding and Lancashire Cheese Hash Browns

1 lb (450 g) Maris Piper potatoes
4 slices of good black pudding
1 egg white
4 oz (110 g) Lancashire cheese
1 teaspoon chopped chives
1 teaspoon chopped parsley
salt and pepper

Leave the potatoes in the skins and cook in boiling water until only just soft. Drain and peel. Grate the potato into a bowl and mix with the herbs. Add a pinch of salt to the egg white, beat with a whisk and mix with the grated potato. Season with salt and pepper. Pat out a quarter of the mix in a circle larger than the black pudding. Place the pudding and 1 oz (25 g) of cheese in the middle. Fold over the potatoes and pat into a circle. Deep fry at 160 C (325 F) until golden brown. Serve with poached egg and Hollandaise sauce.

The River House

Bill Scott

The River House, originally a yeoman farmer's dwelling built in 1836, has an historic setting. In the 16th and 17th centuries Russian ships sailed up the River Wyre to the ports of Skippool and Wardleys bringing grain, cotton and flax. The emigrant ship *Six Sisters* sailed from Skippool to America and here the barque *Hope* was built. There is now a modern Marina but the fame of the River House run by Bill Scott and, before him, by his mother Jean Scott, has spread nation-wide and to Europe.

Bill's suggestions for a three-course meal included: Starter: Hot grapefruit with honey and brandy; Main Course: Posh Hot Pot; Pudding: Syrup sponge with cream custard; Wine: Beaujolais – Moulin à Vent.

Mr Scott kindly gave me the following recipes, the likes of which politician Ted Heath enjoys when he visits The River House.

Poached Scallops

4 good sized king scallops per person

For Poaching Liquid/Sauce
½ pint (300 ml) cream
½ pint (300 ml) white wine
salt and pepper
dill

Remove the rubbish from the scallops especially the little chewey bit on the side. Put the ingredients into a saucepan and bring to the boil. Put in the scallops, bring to the boil again, switch off, leave for 2 minutes and serve.

N.B. The flavour of the sauce is dictated by the type of wine, so dry wine makes dry sauce, medium wine makes medium sauce. Remember that the balance of ingredients is important. Also do not under any circumstances overcook scallops; far better that someone says, "These scallops aren't cooked," than have them stringy and horrible.

Posh Hot Pot

4 noissettes of lamb per person
4 medium sized carrots
1 swede
2 medium onions
4-5 new potatoes per person
2 pints (1200 ml) beef stock
½ pint (300 ml) cooking port
½ pint (300 ml) red wine

Ask your butcher in advance to prepare the noisettes, giving him a couple of days' notice.

Place the noisettes in a baking dish. Top and tail the carrots and cut them into ¼ inch (1 cm) discs. Top and tail the swede, chop in half from top to bottom, with a paring knife remove the skin and the layer of fibre that is just under the skin. Chop the swede.

Skin and chop the onions. Wash and cut the potatoes into 2 or 3 pieces. Distribute the vegetables and potatoes between the noisettes of lamb. Pour the stock and wines over the dish. Cover with foil and cook in a moderate oven for about 2 hours, removing the foil for the last half hour so as to brown the noisettes. Serve with a garnish of your choice.

Ticky Tacky Pudding

8 oz (225 g) stoned dates chopped

2 oz (50 g) chopped walnuts

½ pint (300 ml) boiling water

1 teaspoon vanilla essence

1 teaspoon coffee powder

4 oz (110 g) soft butter

6 oz (175 g) soft brown sugar

8 oz (225 g) self raising flour, sifted

3 eggs

1 teaspoon bicarbonate of soda

Add the dates, vanilla essence and coffee powder to the boiling water. Soak for 10 minutes.

Cream the sugar and butter and slowly add the beaten eggs. Add the flour, bicarbonate of soda, walnuts and the date mixture. Beat slowly until well-mixed. Pour into a lined tin and bake at 158 C (300 F) for about 45 minutes or until firm.

The Sauce

8 oz (225 g) butter

12 oz (350 g) brown sugar

¾ pint (450 ml) cream

Place the butter and sugar into a pan and melt together. Add the cream and bring to the boil. Take off heat and pour over the pudding. Serve with double cream or ice cream.

Andrew Nutter – the Flying Chef

Andrew Nutter has been resident chef on 'Granada Tonight' since January 1998. Of all today's up and coming young chefs, Andrew's approach impresses by virtue of his confidence and whirlwind virtuosity. His Channel 5 series "Utter Nutter" proves that cookery can be good fun. "The Flying Chef" is an apt description and it is no surprise that he has been shortlisted for the BBC. Good Food Awards 'Cooking Personality of the Year'. The Nutter Experience is not just a meal but an adventure. From his restaurant in Edenfield Road, Cheesden, Norden, near Rochdale , Andrew has sent these recipes for a full meal, starting with his "dream fish diet".

Andrew Nutter

Parmesan-crusted Salmon
with a Mussel and Coriander Chowder

4 x 6 oz (175 g) salmon fillets skinned and boned
salt and freshly ground black pepper
small bunch fresh coriander
1 tablespoon olive oil
1 oz (25 g) freshly grated Parmesan

For the Mussel Chowder

2 lbs (1 kg) mussels cleaned

1 tablespoon olive oil

1 rasher smoked bacon, rinded and chopped

1 onion peeled and finely chopped

1 clove garlic peeled and finely chopped

7 fl oz (200 ml) dry white wine

1 carrot peeled and finely diced

1 leek trimmed, finely diced and washed

1 potato peeled and finely diced

7 fl oz (200 ml) whipping cream

1 tablespoon chopped fresh coriander

Pre-heat the oven to 150 C (300 F). Make a horizontal cut half way into each salmon fillet. Lift the top flap, season under it with salt and pepper, lay on a few leaves of coriander and re-form the fillet.

Heat a frying pan and put in the olive oil. Seal the salmon on both sides until it is golden brown. Sprinkle the fish with Parmesan, put it on a baking sheet and bake in the oven for about 10 minutes or until the fish is cooked through. Clean the mussels. Heat the olive oil in a saucepan, add the bacon and fry until it is golden brown, then put in the onion and garlic and cook for 3-4 minutes until slightly softened. Add the mussels to the saucepan, discarding any open ones, pour in the white wine, cover and leave to cook for 2-3 minutes, shaking the pan occasionally until the mussels have opened. Remove them with a slotted spoon, discarding any that are still closed. Keep them warm.

Add the carrot, leek and potato to the white wine and mussel juices in the saucepan and cook for 10-12 minutes until the vegetables are tender.

Now pour in the cream and bring to the boil. Add the chopped coriander, then return the mussels to the pan and warm through until they are sufficiently hot to serve. Over-cooking the mussels at this stage, though, will toughen them, Serve the chunky mussel chowder around the Parmesan-crusted salmon in large soup bowls.

Crisp Bury Black Pudding Won-tons

Won-ton skins are small squares of thin Chinese pastry obtainable from Chinese delicatessen shops.

---

1 tablespoon olive oil

1 small onion peeled and finely chopped

1 clove garlic peeled and finely chopped

1 inch (2.5 cm) piece of fresh ginger, peeled and finely chopped

1 lb (450 g) black pudding skinned and chopped

1 bunch spring onions, about 8, trimmed and finely chopped

5 oz (l50 g) chicken breast, boned and skinned

salt and freshly ground black pepper

1 oz (25 g) butter at room temperature

2 eggs

¼ pint (150 ml) whipping cream

a little freshly ground nutmeg

a few leaves fresh basil, chopped

1 x 12 oz (350 g) packet won-ton skins

egetable oil for deep-frying

Heat the olive oil in a non-stick frying pan and sauté the onion, garlic and ginger. When tley have softened add the black pudding and cook for about a minute. Add the spring onions and remove the pan from the heat so that they remain crunchy. Put it to one side to cool. Take the chicken breast and blend it in a food processor with a teaspoon of salt. Add the butter and blend again. Now add an egg and continue to blend while you pour in the cream. Stop the motor from time to time and scrape the inside of the bowl with a rubber spatula so that everything is evenly combined.

Stir the chicken mousse into the black pudding mixture and season with salt, pepper and nutmeg. Finally add the basil.

Lay out 6-9 won-ton skins on a clean work surface and place a spoonful of the black pudding mixture in the centre of each. Beat the remaining egg and use it to brush the edges of the won-ton skins. Fold each in turn to form a triangle and press the edges firmly together. Repeat until all the mixture has been used. Heat a deep pan of oil to l80 C (350 F). Fry about 6 won-tons at a time until they are golden brown, about 2-3 minutes. Drain and turn them out onto kitchen paper. Serve hot.

Rum-scented Mini Eccles Cakes

4 oz (110 g) currants

4 tablespoons orange liqueur

finely grated zest of ½ orange

6 oz (175 g) puff pastry – use trimmings if you like

1 oz (25 g) butter

1 egg beaten

a little caster sugar for sprinkling

Combine the currants, orange liqueur and zest in a small bowl, cover and leave for 24 hours until the fruit is plump and has absorbed the liqueur. Pre-heat the oven to 160 C (325 F). Roll out the puff pastry until it is nice and thin (it's a good idea to use pastry trimmings as you don't need the pastry to rise) and then cut it into rounds the size of a tumbler, about 2½-2¾ ins (6-7 cm) in diameter. Place a scant teaspoonful of marinated currants in the middle and add a small piece of butter and a sprinkle of sugar. Brush the outer edge of the pastry with the egg, then gather the pastry rim together in the centre and pinch to seal the filling in a small pastry sack. Turn the Eccles cake so that the sealed bit is underneath then roll it gently with a rolling pin, just until the fruit starts to show beneath the pastry and the cake is slightly flattened. Continue until the ingredients are used up. Put the cakes on a baking sheet and brush the tops with a touch more egg. Dust with sugar and make a cut in the top of each. Put them in the oven for about 10 minutes until they are golden brown. Remove from the oven, cool them slightly and serve.

Paul Webster, Clifton Arms, Lytham St. Anne's

The present-day renowned Clifton Arms Hotel, like the Ship Inn and Royal, stands on an historic site. In the early 19th century it was an inn where stage-coaches called. "Charlie's Mast", an old landmark for shipping, stood opposite and the famous windmill had canvas sails. At this hotel, well-known for hospitality and good food, the recently appointed Head Chef, Paul Webster, carries on a great tradition and is well-endowed to do so, coming, as he does, fresh from 10 years' experience in London at Carlton Towers, The Ritz and The Criterion. Paul has also been a chef on board the QE2. Here are two of his recipes.

Twice-baked Lancashire Cheese Soufflé

serves 6

---

1 pint milk (600 ml)

1 small onion

pinch ground nutmeg

3 oz (75 g) butter

3 oz (75 g) plain flour

5 egg yolks

5 egg whites

4 oz (150 g) Lancashire cheese

salt and pepper to taste

Combine the onion, milk and nutmeg in a saucepan and slowly bring to the boil. Melt the butter over a medium heat in a separate saucepan, stirring in the flour to make a roux.

Gradually add the warm milk to the roux, stirring continuously, until a smooth sauce is formed. Allow to cool.

When cool, beat in the egg yolks and grated cheese. Season to taste. In a large bowl, whisk up the egg whites until they form a. smooth, firm peaks, then gently fold in the cheese mixture,

Grease six ramekin moulds with melted butter and dry Parmesan cheese and fill with the prepared mixture.

Place moulds in a large roasting dish half filled with water and cook in a pre-heated oven at 180 C (350 F) for 20-25 minutes. Remove from the oven and allow to cool. Turn souffles out of the moulds onto a clean tray.

Re-heat souffles in a hot oven for 4-5 minutes and serve on a crisp green salad with your favourite salad dressing.

Top Tips

Do not add milk too quickly to the roux to avoid getting a lumpy sauce. Fold the egg whites in gently into the mixture to ensure a light souffle. Do not open the oven door whilst cooking for at least 15 minutes.

Smoked Haddock Fish Cakes

serves 6

2¼ lbs (1 kg) smoked haddock, skinned and boned
18 oz (500 g) mashed potato
2 oz (50 g) finely chopped parsley
1 pint (600 ml) milk
1 bay leaf
salt and pepper to taste
1 teaspoon garlic purée

Coating

1 packet dry white breadcrumbs
flour to coat fishcakes
1 whole egg mixed with a little milk

Paul Webster

Poach the haddock in milk with the bay leaf for 20 minutes. Strain and allow to cool, Combine the mashed potato, fish, parsley, garlic and season to taste. Shape the mixture into 18 golf ball-size cakes. Coat the cakes with the flour, then the egg mixture and lastly the breadcrumbs. Pan fry the cakes in a little butter and oil till golden brown. Finish cooking the cakes in a pre-heated oven at 200 C (400 F) for 10 minutes. Serve 3 to a portion with a green salad and a little flavoured mayonnaise.

Top Tips!

For poaching fish, bring the milk to the boil then allow to sinmmer. When combining ingredients, do not overmix (avoids glue-like texture). When frying, ensure the pan is hot before adding the oil and butter.

David Charnley – The Moorcock

Set in wonderful but wild scenery close to the Trough of Bowland, one can imagine how glad travellers would be to see the lights of this inn especially if the weather was severe. The late George Formby visited and royal visitors have been entertained there. The Moorcock has long enjoyed an enviable reputation for good food and hospitality.

The restored and extended inn is now under the personal supervision of Peter and Susan Fillery, whose Head Chef, David Charnley, has provided the following recipes. Wild and woolly Lancashire might come to mind in such recipes as Pig 'n Pud, yet another brilliant variant on black pudding – and in Pendle, Bowland and Rossendale Forests boars did once roam. At Lower Greystoneley Farm, Leagram, 100% pure boars, brought from an original member of the Wild Boar Association still run in family groups.

The Brass Room in The Moorcock Inn: a century ago, duck and green peas at the famous Moorcock Inn drew crowds from miles around. In fact it was the only main course when Tom Kendall was landlord. Every Spring my grandfather Ned Hoghton and my father journeyed there from Belthorn in a wagonette for this treat. Sampling home-made pea and ham soup before a crackling log fire, we were assured that the Moorcock Inn is still preserving Lancashire cooking.

Here is a competition winner from The Moorcock, which was demonstrated at Claridge's Hotel in London:

Scrooge's Revelation

12 oz (350 g) plain flour

6 oz (175 g) butter

pinch of sugar

pinch of salt

Bind the ingredients together with an egg after rubbing the butter into the flour. Roll out. Line a tin with this pastry and cover the base with a good layer of mincemeat.

The Sponge

6 oz (175 g) margarine

6 oz (175 g) sugar

2 eggs

6 oz (175 g) self raising flour

2 oz (50 g) ground almonds

Cream the sugar and margarine, beat in the eggs then add the flour and ground almonds. Pile the sponge onto the mincemeat and bake for 40 minutes in a moderate oven. Serve warm with double cream.

Stilton Creamy Mushrooms

4 oz (110 g) mature Stilton crumbled

½ pint (300 ml) double cream

8 oz (225 g) button mushrooms cut into quarters

Place the Stilton and cream into a pan and melt for 4-6 minutes then add the quartered mushrooms. Simmer until the.mushrooms are cooked and the cream has thickened. Season gently as this sauce may be salty. Serve with warm, crusty bread.

Shropshire Mushroom Steak

10 oz (275 g) good sirloin steak
4 oz (110 g) Shropshire blue cheese grated
½ oz (15 g) diced onion
3 oz (75 g) sliced mushrooms
seasoning
sprig of thyme
brandy

Cook the onion, mushroom and thyme in a sauté pan and add the brandy. Reduce. Cook the steak to your own liking. Top with the mushroom mixture and add the cheese. Grill until the cheese has melted, then serve.

Traditional Roasted Duckling with Strawberry Sauce and Green Peas

serves 2

1 duckling 4-4½ lbs (2 kg)

Rinse the duckling under cold running water. Remove any loose blood or long stubble. Lightly rub all over with salt. Place the duckling on a trivet of vegetables and add a little water just to cover the trivet. Cook for 3 hours at 200 C (400 F). If a leg of the duck can easily be twisted, then it is ready. Allow to rest for 20 minutes.

Strawberry Sauce

8 oz (225 g) cleaned strawberries cut into quarters
½ glass medium white wine
1 teaspoon butter
1 teaspoon white wine vinegar
1 oz (25 g) chopped onion

In a thick-bottomed pan place the onion, white wine, vinegar and seasoning. Reduce until the liquid has halved. Add the strawberries and simmer for about 5 minutes. When the strawberries are soft and cooked, pass through a sieve into a clean pan. Return to heat, then add the butter to clarify and to disperse scum. Correct the seasoning. If the sauce thickens, add a little chicken stock. Serve with cooked green peas glazed with butter.

The Normandie, Birtle

The Normandie at Elbut Lane, Birtle is idyllically situated near the Pennine scenery of the Cheesden Gorge, yet close to Bury – one of the busiest of Lancashire towns. Taken over by the Moussa family in 1985, it has gained many coveted awards for food, wine and service. The Moussa ideal says it all: "A great meal is a combination of presentation, texture, taste, service, comfort and attention to detail, from buying the freshest and highest quality food to the last piece of garnish." Here is one of their recipes, first devised by Paul Bellingham. Their current Head Chef, Anthony Byrom has kindly assisted by checking over this recipe for an unusual 'Dodine' – a technical term describing the sausage-like shape of the finished dish:

Guinea Fowl Dodine with Bury Black Pudding

Two 3 lb (1.5 kg) guinea fowls
2 Bury black puddings, diced
1 onion, diced finely
1 clove of garlic, crushed
2 tablespoons juices from the cooked guineafowl
8 tablespoons cream
2 tablespoons brandy
1 tablespoon Madeira
salt and pepper

First, debone the guinea fowls: bone each guinea fowl by starting underneath and working up the sides. The skins, legs and breasts must come off whole. Keep all the bones to make the stock (see below). Lay the skins out flat (you need these later) and remove the breasts and legs. Trim and cut the breasts into three equal strips after removing the fillets. Bone and trim the meat from the legs, then mince the leg meat and fillets twice.

You now have to make a highly concentrated stock, called a *jus-lie*. To do this, roast the bones until golden brown. Then fry until golden-brown a quantity of vegetables including carrots, celery, onion, leek and a bulb of garlic. Transfer the cooked bones and vegetables into a pan, cover with water, and boil the mixture for about 4 hours. Skim the fat from the stock and sieve the liquid. Finally, boil to reduce down to about two tablespoons – the end result should be of a Marmite-like colour and thickness.

When cool, add the concentrated stock to the minced meat with the cream, brandy and Madeira. Beat well. Sweat the onions and garlic until soft. Cool and add to the meat mixture. Fry the diced Bury black pudding in a non-stick pan until slightly crisp. Cool, then add to the meat and season.

Lay out the guinea fowl skin and place half the meat mixture in a line along it, approximately 1 ½- 2 ins (4 - 5 cm) in width. Place the strips of meat in a line along the minced meat and place the rest of the meat mixture on top of these strips. Place the second skin on top of the meat. Push down and trim the skin, making sure there is enough skin to overlap.

Place the dodine (see above) onto a greased tin foil and roll tightly into a long sausage shape. Place onto a wire rack and roast in a hot oven at 220 C (425 F) until the juices run clear. Remove and cool. Slice when cold and serve with a kumquat relish.

The Caprice Tea Shop

Peter and Lindsey Jenkinson, proprietors of the Caprice Tea Shop, Moor Lane, Clitheroe, a member of the highly esteemed Guild of Tea Shops, are dedicated to the best in home cooking. With a family tradition going back generations, they offer Lancashire fare such as Tatty Pot, Salamgundy, Colne Bacon and Egg Flan and Burnley Stew as well as a magnificent display of oven-fresh, home made confectionery. They also have what must be the largest private collection of recipe books around, running to over 2,000. For their Wakes Week Promotion, which attracted visitors from as far away as Australia and New Zealand, they won the Tea Council's Media Promotion Award. Lindsey has provided recipes for two of the highlights which feature regularly in their bill of fare.

Hindle Wakes Chicken

4 chicken breast fillets
4 slices streaky bacon
1 oz (25 g) butter
4 ready soaked prunes, chopped
2 oz (50 g) breadcrumbs
1 small onion, finely chopped
1 pinch thyme
1 pinch basil
1 lemon
1 teaspoon fresh parsley, chopped
½ pint (300 ml) chicken stock
small tub of single cream
1 tablespoon cornflour
salt and pepper

Wash the lemon, pare half and reserve half. Simmer the parings in a little water to extract the flavour, squeeze the juice from the lemon half and strain the parings into the lemon juice. Discard the parings. Place the breadcrumbs, prunes, onions, juice and herbs into a basin. Mix and season well.

Take the chicken breast fillets and make a slit in each one to form a pocket. Fill each pocket with the prepared stuffing and wrap a piece of bacon round the chicken and secure with a cocktail stick.

Heat the butter in a frying pan and brown the chicken lightly on each side. When this is achieved, transfer to a casserole dish and deglaze the frying pan with the chicken stock. Pour over the chicken and cook for 30 minutes at 180 C (350 F).

Mix the cornflour with a little water. Take the chicken out of the casserole and keep warm. Remove the cocktail sticks. Add the cornflour mixture to the stock and thicken. When this is achieved, add the cream and spoon the sauce over the chicken breast. Use the other half of the lemon to decorate together with the fresh parsley.

Strawberry, Apple and Almond Tart

1 punnet strawberries
1 small Bramley apple
2 oz (50 g) caster sugar

The Pastry

4 oz (110 g) plain flour
2 oz (50 g) butter
1 oz (25 g) icing sugar
1 egg yolk

The Almond Filling

3 oz (75 g) self raising flour
6 oz (175 g) softened butter
6 oz (175 g) caster sugar
3 size 2 eggs
3 oz (75 g) ground almonds
a few drops almond essence

Using a food processor, place the flour, butter and icing sugar in the bowl with the pastry blade attachment and process until the mixture resembles breadcrumbs. Add the egg yolk and continue until the mixture comes together into a ball, then rest the pastry in the fridge for half an hour. Hull and wash the strawberries, reserving 4, and cut the rest into slices. Peel and core the apple and cut into slices. Roll out the pastry and line a 10 inch (25.5 cm) loose-bottomed flan tin. Spread the fruit on the bottom and sprinkle with caster sugar. Again using the food processor, put in the butter, caster sugar, eggs, ground almonds, essence and flour and process until everything is incorporated. Spread the almond mixture evenly over the fruit and sprinkle with flaked almonds. Bake at 180 C (350 F). When cool, take out of the flan ring, dredge with icing sugar and decorate with the reserved strawberries.

Riverbank Cafe

Roy and Julia Greenwood of the Riverbank Cafe, Slaidburn, also known as The Cafe on the Green, well deserve their reputation for home-made food. This popular Lancashire tea shop with wonderful views across the river also has an interesting history in that the upper floor used to be a coffin maker's shop. Julia provided this information for one of her specialities.

Chicken in a Creamy Ham and Mushroom Sauce

Fry boneless, skinless chicken in a pan to seal the meat and place in a baking dish. Fry the mushrooms in butter and garlic. Add salt and pepper. Put this with the chicken, retaining the butter. Add more butter and make a roux sauce. Add cream to the sauce and pour the sauce over the chicken. Remove fat from the boiled ham and chop the ham up finely and add this. Cover the baking dish with foil and bake at 180 C (350 F) until the chicken is cooked. When ready to serve, scatter chopped parsley over it.

Tips from the Top

🍴 The great chef Marcel Boulestin believed that "peace and happiness begin where garlic is used in cooking".

🍴 Do not store garlic in the refrigerator.

🍴 Bury 3 peeled and pressed garlic cloves in half a cup of sea salt. Remove the garlic and use the salt as seasoning.

🍴 When cooking vegetables add several whole cloves of garlic into the water. This lends a subtle aroma.

🍴 The small cloves of garlic often produce the most flavour. Avoid burning garlic as it can singe much more quickly than onion. Burning results in bitter flavour.

🍴 To remove the odour of garlic from the hands, wash with lemon juice.

🍴 When cooking pasta, use three times the amount of water as pasta.

🍴 Salt the water. Add a teaspoon of olive oil. Add the pasta to boiling water and cook until al dente i.e. the outside is soft but it is firm in the centre. Drain the pasta very well and mix your favourite sauce into the pasta before serving.

🍴 To avoid a black ring round egg yolks, the eggs should be put into boiling water and boiled for exactly 10 minutes. Slightly salt the water and prick the blunt end of the egg with a fine needle. Cool under cold water and they shell easily.

🍴 Before stuffing a bird wrap the herbs (thyme, tarragon etc.) in muslin dipped in oil. Remove the muslin bag before carving.

🍴 Soak a lettuce in iced water for a few minutes.

🍴 Never remove the stalks from strawberries before cleaning or the water will penetrate and make them mushy. Shake carefully in damp muslin. Ten minutes before serving, sprinkle them with lemon juice.

🍴 To make extra light Béchamel Sauce, stir the white of an egg, beaten to a froth, into the cream before adding the cream to the mixture.

🍴 Have a good supply of oven cloths. Keep them dry and spotless, cleansing daily any which have been in use. This eliminates burns and fatty smells.

● When boiling freshly dug young beetroots, retain tops and roots, otherwise they "bleed" and lose their distinctive colour. Once cooked, the skin slides off easily.

● Shelled hazel nuts, toasted whole in the oven, are excellent with ice cream and fruit. The skins rub off easily when gently roasted.

● A warmed knife blade should be used to cut iced cakes or meringues as it prevents dragging.

● A handy way to separate eggs is by placing an egg cup over the yolk. Tilt the plate to drain off the white.

● Egg whites can be whisked into jelly on the point of setting or used as meringue topping for milk pudding.

● Pastry cooked in glass oven-ware should be stood on a bright metal sheet in the oven. This ensures well-done quiches and custards as the heat is conducted through the metal.

● Gather fruit for jam or jelly making on a dry day.

● Raspberries are improved by adding ¼ pint (150 ml) of redcurrant juice to every pound (450 g) of fruit.

● Heavy cast iron and thick earthenware slow cook to perfection and bring out all the flavour.

Acknowledgements

First and foremost to my patient husband: chauffeur; adviser; food taster and sternest critic.

Many people have helped, including family and friends. I especially thank the following:

Elaine A. Barnes, Catering Co-Ordinator, Blackburn Cathedral

Paul Bellingham, former Head Chef, The Normandie, Birtle

Alison Brown, Radio Lancashire

Carol Burrow

Anthony Byrom, Head Chef, The Normandie, Birtle

Ian M.T. Carter, Chef

David Chamley, Head Chef, The Moorcock Inn

W. and M. Gibson, Bakers and Confectioner

The Guild of Conservation Grade Producers

John Gledhill, Chef

Roy and Julia Greenwood

Margaret Hacking

Paul Heathcote, Chef, Heathcote's Restaurant

Peter and Lindsey Jenkinson, The Riverside Cafe, Slaidburn

Ros and Chris Johnson, Ramsbottom Organics

Bill Jordan, Chairman, W. Jordan Ltd

Dot Little, Caterer, Alston Hall

M.M. Moussa, The Normandie Hotel and Restaurant

North West Fine Foods

Andrew Nutter, Nutter's Restaurant

Bill Scott, The River House, Skippool

Jim Watson, Master Butcher

Paul Webster, Head Chef, The Clifton Arms, Lytham

Graham Wilkinson, Principal, Alston Hall Residential College.

Index

BEST TEA SHOP WALKS IN LANCASHIRE
Clive Price
Walk through breathtaking upland scenery, lush river valleys and along impressive coastal paths and complete your day by indulging in the celebrated English pastime of afternoon tea.This refreshing blend of walks and tea shops helps you get the very best out of Lancashire. £6.95

BEST PUB WALKS IN LANCASHIRE
Neil Coates
Join local author Neil Coates in a celebration of the best pubs, beers and walks in wonderful countryside. Tried and tested country inns welcome weary walkers. £6.95

DISCOVERY WALKS IN LANCASHIRE
Brian Conduit
30 routes of varying lengths and terrain, suitable both for seasoned walkers and casual family strollers. All walks have a heritage theme and enable you to appreciate both Lancashire's rich historical legacy as well as its ever-changing landscape. £6.95

WALKS IN MYSTERIOUS LANCASHIRE
Graham Dugdale
Delving into a host of mysterious places throughout Lancashire, this unusual collection of 30 walks, suitable for all the family, appeals to walkers with enquiring minds. £6.95

50 CLASSIC WALKS IN LANCASHIRE
Terry Marsh
Terry Marsh reveals Lancashire at its diverse best - from wild woodland expanses and witch country, to tranquil river valleys. £7.95

WEST LANCASHIRE WALKS / EAST LANCASHIRE WALKS *(2 Volumes)*
Michael Smout
No need to venture into touristy areas, it's all on the doorstep for Lancashire's walkers - "Knowledgeable guide to 25 rambles by the Ramblers' West Lancs Group Chairman" RAMBLING TODAY. £6.95 per volume

BY-WAY BIKING IN LANCASHIRE
Henry Tindell
From Morecambe Bay to Bolton and from

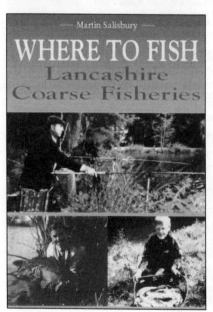

Blackpool to Burnley, Henry Tindell reveals Lancashire's outstanding potential as a destination for mountain bikers. £7.95

CHILLING TRUE TALES OF OLD LANCASHIRE
Keith Johnson
Set in Victorian Lancashire, here is a spine-chilling collection of tales - "...sure to thrill, chill and amaze" THE LANCASTER GUARDIAN. £6.95

LANCASHIRE MAGIC & MYSTERY: Secrets of the Red Rose County
Kenneth Fields
Covering all of Lancashire, including Merseyside and Greater Manchester, Ken Field's new book will guide you to places of mystery and curiosity. £6.95

WHERE TO FISH: LANCASHIRE COARSE FISHERIES
Martin Salisbury
The definitive guide to angling in Lancashire - places on your doorstep and others you've never heard of! Covers 113 fisheries - including stillwaters, rivers and canals. Full details of species, rules, tickets, costs and access for each fishery. £6.95

TOWNS & VILLAGES OF BRITAIN: LANCASHIRE
Michael Smout
The moors, valleys and mossland of Lancashire are the backdrop to this account of the county's towns and villages. Michael Smout is keen to emphasise that Lancashire's austere mill towns often obscure a rich, often eerie past. "The histories of our towns and villages neatly gathered in one definitive guide" SOUTHPORT VISITER. £8.95

All of our books are available through booksellers. In case of difficulty, or for a free catalogue, please contact:
SIGMA LEISURE,
1 SOUTH OAK LANE, WILMSLOW,
CHESHIRE SK9 6AR.
Phone: 01625-531035
Fax: 01625-536800.
E-mail: info@sigmapress.co.uk
Web site: http//www.sigmapress.co.uk
MASTERCARD and VISA orders welcome.